D1361738

63535

Roberts, John Morris, 1928-
    The world of Greece and Rome / J. M. Roberts
; design, Arthur Lockwood ; illustration
research, Diana Phillips ; text research,
Nicola Sissons. Harmondsworth, England :
Penguin Books, c1980.
    128 p. : ill. (An Illustrated world
history / J. M. Roberts ; 3)

1. Civilization, Greek. 2. Rome -
Civilization. I. Title.
0140640037   1175440

6/he

An Illustrated
World History

1 The Earliest Men and Women
2 The First Civilizations
3 The World of Greece and Rome
4 Different Worlds
5 Making One World
6 One World: Europe the Maker
7 One World: Disappearing Barriers
8 The Age of Upheaval: The World Since 1914

J. M. Roberts was educated in Somerset and at Keble College, Oxford. From 1953 to 1979 he was a Fellow and Tutor in Modern History of Merton College, Oxford. During that time he paid several visits to the United States, and held visiting professorships at the Universities of South Carolina and Columbia. He edited the extremely successful partwork publication, Purnell's *History of the Twentieth Century*; and in 1976 brought out his one-volume *History of the World* to great acclaim. In 1979 he was appointed Vice-Chancellor of Southampton University.

An Illustrated
World History
3

Design: Arthur Lockwood
Illustration research: Diana Phillips
Text research: Nicola Sissons

J. M. Roberts

The World of Greece and Rome

Penguin Books

Introduction

In these books the early story of mankind has so far had to ramble all over the globe, from China to Central America. Now, for something like a thousand years, it can be pinned down much more closely in space. The area involved is still large, but pretty well defined on the map. It covers (roughly speaking) the lands all round the Mediterranean, including the Levant, Syria, Europe as far east as the Rhine and Danube, and the fringe of the Black Sea.

Of course, this part of the world was never cut off from what went on outside. Ideas, knowledge, customs and (perhaps most important of all) peoples flowed into it from the north and east and changed its life very much as time passed. Yet the peoples living in this zone grappled with and sometimes welcomed the forces pressing on them from the outside. Often they made something quite new of them. They could do this because they were not overwhelmed by them; they had a civilization of their own to be proud of and which was to have more effect on the history of the world than any other until modern times.

It was founded in the Aegean by the people we call Greeks between about 700 and 350 BC. Civilization can grow, and can change in growing, and what the Greeks left behind was added to enormously later on, but their traditions and achievements (or many of them) were admired and treasured by the Romans, who tried to spread them over the largest empire ever to be based on the Mediterranean world. The Romans too, by making it Christian, added something else to that civilization from the East. Christianity grew out of the thought and traditions of the Jews, an eastern people.

Greeks, Romans, Jews: they were the founders of much we still take for granted. And they shaped so much of the story of mankind that this book will be about little else. This is not because important things were not going on elsewhere in the world between 1000 BC and AD 500. It is simply more convenient to describe this civilization as a whole, without breaking up its story for more than a glance at what was going on elsewhere, important though that is in its place.

Published by Penguin Books Ltd
Harmondsworth, Middlesex, England

Copyright © 1980 by J. M. Roberts

Design and illustration research by IKON
25 St Pancras Way, London NW1

First published 1980

ISBN 064.003 7

Phototypeset by
Oliver Burridge & Co. Ltd, Crawley

Printed in Great Britain by
Hazell Watson & Viney Ltd, Aylesbury, Bucks

Contents

page 4 Introduction

    6 The setting

  10 Greece

  12 The Dark Age in Greece

  14 Hellas

  18 *Homer's* Odyssey

  22 Greeks overseas

  24 Great powers

  28 The Etruscans and early Rome

  32 The *polis*

  36 The Persian wars

  40 How the Greeks lived

  46 The Greek miracle

  52 *The Greek theatre*

  54 The Peloponnesian war

  55 *Democracy in Athens*

  58 Alexander the Great and his legacy

page 64 The rise of Roman power

  70 The decay of the Republic

  74 *The first invasion of Britain*

  76 *The first emperors*

  80 The coming of Christianity

  86 Other civilizations

  94 The Roman empire

100 *Pompeii*

104 Christianity and the empire

108 Parthians and Persians

112 The imperial frontiers

116 Diocletian and Constantine

120 Decline in the West

122 Conclusion

123 Time chart

124 Acknowledgements

125 Index

Title-page pictures : men and women of the ancient world. Left to right : bronze statue of a Greek charioteer from about 470 BC; portrait on a mummy case of an Egyptian woman from the second century AD; head of a Syrian woman in limestone from about 50 BC; head of a Pompeian banker in bronze from about AD 70.

The setting

From a geographer's point of view the Mediterranean is very self-contained. Almost everywhere its coasts are closely backed up by high hills and mountains; the land drops away from them to narrow coastal plains, often with dramatic suddenness. The main exception is in Libya and Egypt, where the shores give way to desert close inland. The Black Sea, which is a sort of spare tank from which water flows into the Mediterranean, has mountainous southern and eastern shores but to the north it lies open to the great plains of Russia from which long rivers roll for hundreds of kilometres towards it. The Danube drains south-eastern and central Europe into the Black Sea too. The Mediterranean itself, though, has only three really important rivers flowing directly into it: the Nile, the longest

of them all, the Rhône, running down through the middle of France with water from the Alps, and the Ebro which runs through the broad valley of Aragon, in Spain. The last great river-system which we need to remember is that of the Po valley, in north Italy, which empties into the Adriatic.

The reason for beginning with the map is that geography has always settled much of what would happen when man became civilized. This has already been shown to be true of other areas in the ancient past, such as Egypt, or the plains of north-western India. It shaped Mediterranean civilization, too.

Climate is another important force. It is not only a matter of very slow, long-term changes like those of prehistory, or of the ups and downs of a few bad years followed by a few good, but

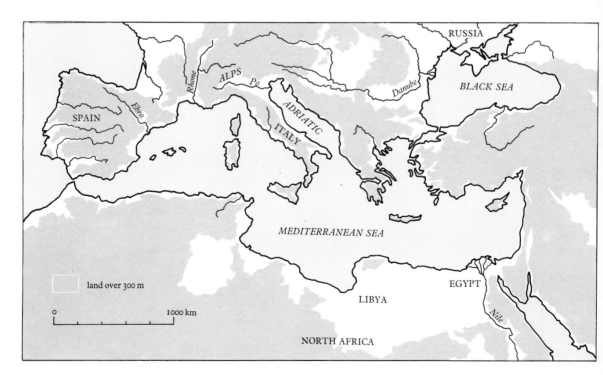

land over 300 m

0   1000 km

RUSSIA
BLACK SEA
Rhône
ALPS
Po
Danube
SPAIN
Ebro
ADRIATIC
ITALY
MEDITERRANEAN SEA
EGYPT
LIBYA
Nile
NORTH AFRICA

High on a hillside overlooking the bay at Cape Sounion, where the land falls away dramatically to the sea, the Greeks built a temple to Poseidon, the sea god.

of the broad shape given by it to human life over hundreds of years. For the most part the Mediterranean lands are warm (but not too warm) and get reasonable rainfall on their hills. In ancient times most of them looked better than they do now, for many of the hills have been stripped by grazing of their cover of trees and bushes, and this has led to the washing away of topsoil.

Two thousand five hundred years ago the coasts would have been much greener: even in North Africa farming went on a fair way inland, the desert being held at bay farther off than nowadays. What we think of as typical North African landscape – dry, stony, sun-burnt – has only come into existence in the last 1500 years or so.

Geography and climate made very much the same sort of life possible all round the Mediterranean. On the narrow plains people grew wheat and barley, and farther up the slopes vines and olives; on the hills they herded sheep and goats. They lived much in the open air, because the climate was not fiercely cold except in the mountains in winter. As well as having so much in common, the peoples of the Mediterranean were tied together as time passed by the sea itself, because communication across it was easier than by land. This meant that when new influences appeared in any part of the Mediterranean they soon spread farther and more quickly than in the land-locked empires of the East.

Now we need to look at one part of the map more closely. North of Crete, between Greece and modern Turkey lies the Aegean Sea. This shares much of the topography and climate of the Mediterranean area as a whole but also has a number of special qualities of its own. For one thing, the coastal plains and the valley floors formed by the rivers from the mountains are smaller here than farther west; the coast is craggier and more indented with little harbours and refuges. The sea itself is full

Above: somewhere before 600 BC the Greeks began to use money, but they still lived in a world whose economics rested on agriculture – as this ear of wheat on a coin from one of their settlements in southern Italy reminds us.

Right: harvesting olives: a Greek vase from about 500 BC.

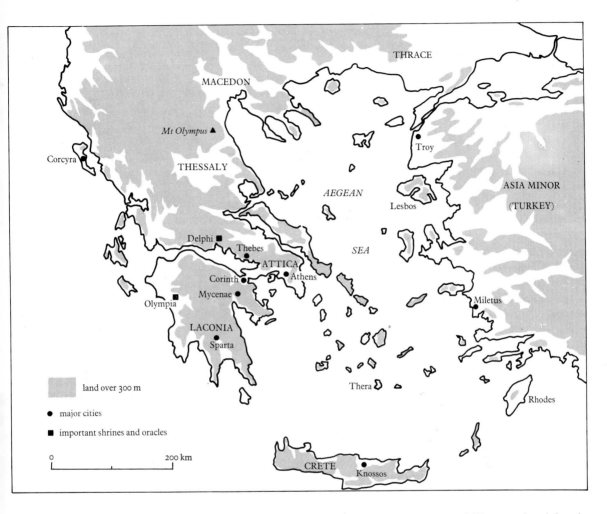

of islands, many of them mere rocks incapable of growing anything, but others very fertile.

Distances across and around this sea are short. Storms and strong prevailing winds make navigation awkward except by certain routes, but even in Minoan times men could sail about it from place to place with some ease once they understood its conditions. This encouraged trade. With trade came other influences. Close at hand to the east and south, in Mesopotamia, Syria and Egypt, lay great civilizations. Even by 2000 BC these areas already had centuries of Bronze Age culture behind them. As early as Minoan times they were

passing on ideas and skills to the island-dwellers and coastal villages of the Aegean. Natural boundaries of deserts and mountains shut off these old civilizations from much contact with India, Central Asia and China, but through the ports of the Levant and the Nile delta they were easily reached from the Aegean. As for the world which lay west of it, there was little to be learnt from the peoples of western Europe by others until at least 500 BC. They supplied metals and a few other raw materials to the richer lands of the Near East, but this was the only contribution they made to eastern Mediterranean civilization.

Greece

Mainland Greece provides the western wall of the Aegean. Behind its straggling, rocky, indented coast lies a land which can be thought of in three main parts. In the south lies a big peninsula called the Peloponnese. This is attached by a very narrow neck (the isthmus of Corinth) to another, still larger, peninsula which broadens northwards from its tip in what is called Attica to the highlands of Thessaly. Finally there is the far north, the mountainous area which runs from Thessaly across to Macedonia.

Geography has always made Greece a difficult country to invade by land, except by a very few routes. To attack it from the sea is easier – but, of course, requires command of the sea first. In very ancient times agriculture spread from the Levant to Macedonia and the islands of the Aegean; it spread by sea and perhaps this means that people who settled in Greece came that way too. But of the Neolithic people who occupied the Greek mainland slowly between about 5000 and 2500 BC we do not know much except that they left to Greek-speakers a few words from their language. The later Greeks called them Pelasgoi, and they were still to be found in some places in the northern Aegean as late as 500 BC

The first 'invaders' of Greece of whose origins we can be sure came from the north, and they appear somewhere about 2500 BC. They were Indo-European tribes of warlike, sheep-herding people who knew how to use chariots. Their societies gave much more importance to males than females (to judge by the contrast between the relics of their religion and the cults much more centred on female deities prevalent in the Near East and the Aegean before their arrival). They pressed steadily southwards, both on the mainland and across the sea. By about 2000 BC these peoples were beginning to penetrate southern Greece, building fortress-settlements to dominate the little plains of fertile land they came across. Some of them spoke languages which were the basis of modern Greek. They can be conveniently called 'Achaeans', the name given by later Greeks to their remote forebears, and they founded the civilization we call 'Mycenaean' (after its biggest centre, at Mycenae). This was a big advance on anything previously to be found in Greece (though not so advanced as that of Minoan Crete) and it lasted a long time – five or six hundred years after its first appearance in about 1600 BC. Its power and influence spread out to sea after a time, to Crete in particular, but to the Levant too. In about 1300 BC Hittite kings were writing to the king of Mycenae and treating him as a person of some importance and usefulness. Palaces found in Cyprus are built much in the style of those of the Mycenaeans.

This bronze dagger was found at Mycenae. The picture on it of a lion hunt is in gold and silver.

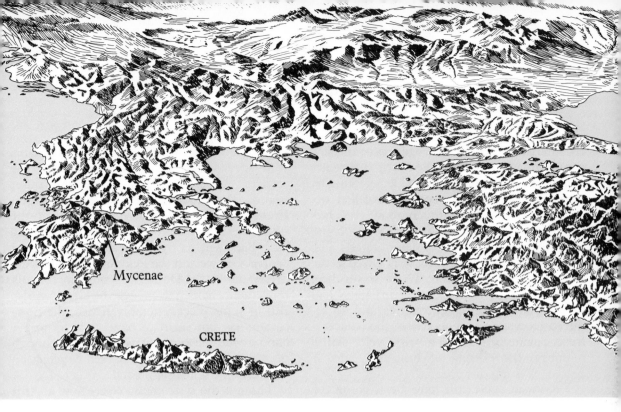

Rocky inlets and mountainous country make Greece a difficult country to invade.

But its spectacular palace buildings and fine gold objects can easily put Mycenaean culture in a false perspective. The first Mycenaeans at least must have been a pretty barbaric lot, not much superior to the people they already found in Greece except in fighting-power (where, no doubt, their chariots helped). They became civilized only after they settled down, and this was almost certainly because of the contacts with Asia which then became possible. True, we have records on tablets to show us that some of the palace centres of Mycenaean civilization had bureaucrats running some of their affairs. But this may not mean much more than that old traditions of acting on a tribal or family basis under the headship of kings had been somewhat stepped up in scale – they were landlords who had discovered the merits of good book-keeping, as it were. Such records need not mean that they had very complicated political arrangements; it is most likely that they were ruled by local

kings advised by councils of headmen. They were not like the eastern empires, with big civil services and complex archives, but more like large estates, one of which belonged to a king whose prestige or power made him accepted by others as a kind of overlord.

Mycenaean civilization did not leave much visible mark on future Greek life, though a number of the palace centres later became the sites of famous Greek cities. Some historical myths and traditions may have lingered on in the songs later sung by Greek bards and handed down the generations by word of mouth, and we know that some early form of Greek was in use in many places in the peninsula in Mycenaean times. The Mycenaeans also pioneered a way of life for later Greeks when they set out to sea, establishing themselves or trading all over the Aegean and the Levant, so it was not unreasonable for their successors to look back hundreds of years later and see them as the first real Greeks.

The Dark Age in Greece

By 1000 BC the Mycenaean age was over. New invaders had come from the north. There is a feeling of collapse about the evidence found by archaeologists for what is sometimes called (because we do not know much about it) 'Dark Age' Greece – roughly from 1000–700 BC. Everything seems to have deteriorated. The new peoples were clearly not so civilized as the Mycenaeans had become. There was a drop in population; perhaps the disturbances had wiped out farming communities and so reduced food supply. The arts of the palaces – fresco painting, building with very skilful masonry, the cutting of beautiful gems – ceased. Writing disappeared.

Yet much must still have been going on. Potters did not stop potting, smiths forging or farmers tilling the ground where they could. In Dark Age Greece we have an example of the way in which human culture builds up reserves as civilization develops so that it can withstand enormous strains. Though civilized societies often fall backwards from their triumphs, they have much knowledge and experience to draw on when they do so, and total regression to barbarism is unlikely except in limited areas. This should hearten us. Even after a nuclear war the wretched survivors would not have to re-invent steam-engines, fishnets or screwdrivers from scratch.

The new invaders were Greek-speakers, but we must not think of them as a united people; they formed a large number of raiding parties and little groups of settlers, at most only subdivisions of clans. They did not all speak the same kind of Greek, but different and strongly marked dialects. This has helped later scholars to trace the outlines of the folk-movements of the Dark Ages. One tribe or clan, seemingly even tougher than the rest, eventually dominated most of the southern Peloponnese –

later called Laconia. These were the Dorians, who spread out from the mainland to be settlers of Rhodes, Cos, Crete and other islands, their dialect marking their advance. From language too we learn that Ionia, on the south-western coast of Asia Minor, seems to have been settled by Achaean fugitives from central Greece and the Peloponnese who were driven out by the Dorians. In this way the folk movements helped to enlarge the Greek world. But in some places, notably Attica, the newcomers do not seem to have had the upper hand (to judge again by language), even though the way of life which had marked Mycenaean civilization itself disappeared.

Though the outcome is clear, how all this happened is still hard to understand. It is very difficult to put together any chronological account of what happened in the Aegean between about 1000 and 700 BC, or to say what caused it. The most important result was the dispersion of Greek-speakers around the Aegean in firmly settled and well-established communities which were the start of hundreds of later Greek cities. Except for Laconia and Attica, which were ruled as regions containing several little cities, each of them was small – even tiny – and independent. They were, to use a word the Greeks invented, 'autonomous', or self-governing, not a part of anybody else's empire. During the Dark Ages they grew in size until some (though only the biggest) may have had ten thousand or more inhabitants. Usually they had a high place or 'Acropolis' as their centre and the home of the shrines of the city gods, and were ruled by 'kings' (of whom the first were probably the leaders of war bands or pirate gangs) who were later replaced by councils of the most important landowners. Here was one difference from Mycenae, whose centres were not really towns but palaces, and this difference affected later Greece.

These little cities could almost always feed themselves on what they grew on the land around them. But, as trade began to revive after the collapse caused by the Dorian invasions, enterprising men began to venture abroad. Gradually they put together again the old networks of commerce which had tied the Aegean together in Mycenaean times.

Some of the things they traded were transported in pots and jars. The skill of potters seems to have been more advanced in mainland Greece than in Ionia. Design and finish had gone badly downhill at the end of the Mycenaean period, but somewhere around 1000 BC pottery was beginning to be made in a new and very exciting style. Athens may have been the place where this started. It was at first very simple, even primitive, stuff, but it was pleasing to the eye, decorated with abstract patterns – lines, concentric circles and bands of colour. For this reason scholars call this pottery 'geometric'. It is often very beautiful and as it developed it became much more complicated. It was not until the eighth century BC, after about 250 years, that this style began to show human figures, and they too were at first drawn in a very geometrical and abstract way.

This pottery reveals growing wealth, the spread of influences from the mainland and reviving trade. All these things mean that life in the Aegean was again becoming more complicated – more civilized, in fact. The ships on some of the vases of the eighth century tell the same story; an Aegean dominated by Greeks was in existence by about 750 BC.

The figures on this large geometric pot suggest that it was made at the end of the Dark Ages in Greece, about 750 BC. Such pots were often set to mark graves in Athens.

Below: detail from the pot above, showing how the human figures (appropriately enough, attending a funeral) were drawn in the same geometrical style as the patterns.

Hellas

In much later times than those we have so far dealt with, the Greeks had a calendar beginning in 776 BC. They counted from that year just as we count from the birth of Christ. It was, they thought, the date of the first Olympic Games, which took their name from the place in western Greece where they were held – Olympia. The Greeks may not have got the date quite right (scholars have questioned the year and it seems, in any case, that an older festival of some sort lay behind these boxing, running, singing and dancing events) but it is a good marker for the beginning of real Greek history. The Olympic Games were the most important of several similar gatherings and went on being held more or less continuously every four years for about a thousand years. Though by about 200 BC they had become in the main a professional show and a big attraction to tourists from other countries, teams of amateurs from all over Greece long represented their cities at them. For most of this time the Olympic Games was the only festival which regularly brought Athenians, Thebans, Spartans and the representatives of many more cities together as Greeks.

The great stadium at Delphi. Like the Olympic Games, the games at Delphi were held every four years.

One of the most exciting spectacles at the games was the chariot race; the charioteers had to be extremely skilled even to finish the course.

The pankration, shown on this Greek drinking vessel, was a combination of boxing and wrestling, with very few holds barred. Most Greek games were contested in the nude; the Greeks thought that nudity fostered pride in an athletic body.

Right: long-jumping on a Greek vase. The jumper carries weights in his hands, which he swings to give him momentum.

Language and literature

The word 'Greeks' comes from Latin, the language of the Romans, not of the Greeks themselves. They called themselves 'Hellenes', a word which by the end of the Dark Ages applied to many different Aegean communities who felt they belonged to the same race. In some important ways they were one people, however much they might quarrel among themselves. The most important thing they had in common was that they were Greek-speakers; they shared a language. What is more, in the eighth century BC that language was just about to develop in a new way. It had first been written down hundreds of years earlier in scripts which have not yet been completely deciphered. So far as we know, it was used then only for accounting, for that is what tablets found at Knossos and in Mycenaean palaces seem to show. But Greek took the written form in which, by and large, it still remains today when the Greeks borrowed the Phoenician alphabet and adapted it to their own needs. The first inscription which has been found in the new Greek characters is on a jug of about 725 BC.

When a language is written down, it begins to evolve in a quite different way. Writing leads to 'standardization' – a growth in the use of a few common words and forms instead of many different local varieties – and better understanding between the speakers of different dialects. Communication over larger areas becomes much easier with written messages. The writing down of their language was therefore another step in the growth of the idea that for all their differences, Greeks had much in common. The Greeks felt this so strongly that their word for a non-Greek was based on the idea that he could not speak Greek: he was *barbaraphonoi* – someone making an unintelligible noise like 'bar-bar-bar' – and this is the word from which we take our word for an uncivilized person, 'barbarian'.

Written language also pins down thought. For centuries bards and story-tellers must have been repeating the tales, songs and legends of the peoples from whom the Greeks had sprung. The outlines of memorized 'literature' of this sort are often very enduring, but details are likely to change as those who are telling the stories or singing the songs try to bring out a point that seems especially apt, or to introduce an allusion which will make performance more effective. When such tales are written down, they are fixed more firmly; there is less room for individuals to alter them. No doubt there were already hundreds of well-known tales about gods and heroes in Dark Age Greece. One group of stories, though, became central to later Greek culture and education because the first written works of Greek literature were taken from them. These were the stories and legends of an Achaean expedition to Troy, a city in Asia Minor, which provided the background to the long poems we call the *Iliad* and the *Odyssey*, two of the greatest works of literature in any language.

Altogether they are about 28,000 lines long. The first gets its title from the Greek name for Troy – Ilium – whose siege is going on while the poem tells us, essentially, about only a few days in the life of a great Achaean hero, Achilles. The second poem is called after its hero, Odysseus, and tells of his ten years' a-wandering after the end of the siege in which he had taken part, of his marvellous adventures and the resourcefulness he showed in them, of his homecoming at last and triumph over those who had tried to usurp his place while he was away. Traditionally these poems were thought to have been written by one man, a blind poet called Homer, who may have lived on the isle of Chios, but this is only one of many disputed facts about them.

Whoever wrote them down first, it is agreed that these poems were written versions of very old material, containing ideas and scraps of fact from many centuries, jumbled together without any sense of what was historically appropriate. A very rough parallel might be to imagine a poem about Christopher Columbus's discovery of America in which, though he travelled in sailing-ships, he was assumed to have a radio, and he would be shown meeting natives who dressed, spoke and thought like Spaniards. This mixed-up material has given scholars plenty of opportunity to argue about what different passages might refer to. Often it turns out that reality must have been very different from what the poem describes. The great ten-year siege of Troy, for example, was probably more like a swift Viking raid by a few hundred freebooters on a little settlement no more than three or four hectares in extent. Still, there are some details mixed up in the poems which are interesting for the light they throw on the Dark Age.

But this was not why they were important to the Greeks. For them, what Homer 'wrote' was somewhat like the Bible for the Jews and early Christians. His texts contained their ancient history, information about their gods and the way they were related to humans and were likely to behave, explanations of human destiny and the purpose of life, guidance on ethics, good breeding, the qualities which made for a good life and much else. Homer was the most important single expression of the things which made the Greeks think of themselves as different from other men. In the *Iliad* and *Odyssey* they could find texts to settle disputes, standards by which to judge behaviour and the most splendid example of how their language could be used. These poems helped form their ideas and tastes for hundreds of years. In later times professional reciters were given large sums to go round reciting them, and, if you had an education at all, it was grounded in the works of Homer. Significantly the Greeks usually referred to him not by his name but simply as '*the* Poet'.

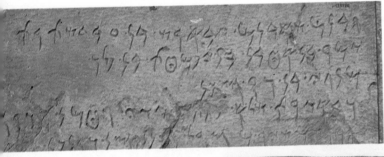

Above: through its development by the Greeks the Phoenician script became the direct ancestor of all western writing. This Phoenician inscription comes from a Tunisian tomb built in the third century BC.

Right: a board inscribed with six lines of Homer, written in late Greek characters. It has an iron handle and may have been used in schools, perhaps being passed round the class.

Homer's Odyssey

During their wanderings, Odysseus and his crew visited the land of the Cyclopes, giant one-eyed creatures, one of whom imprisoned them in his cave and proceeded to eat them, two at a time, for breakfast and supper. But the resourceful Odysseus formed a plan. One night, the giant got drunk. Now read on, in Odysseus' account :

'He toppled over and fell face upward on the floor, where he lay with his great neck twisted to one side, conquered, as all men are, by sleep. His drunkenness made him vomit, and a stream of wine mixed with morsels of men's flesh poured from his throat. I went at once and thrust our pole deep under the ashes of the fire to make it hot, and meanwhile gave a word of encouragement to all my men, to make sure that no one should play the coward and leave me in the lurch. When the fierce glow from the olive stake warned me that it was about to catch alight in the flames, green as it was, I withdrew it from the fire and brought it over to the spot where my men were standing ready. Heaven now inspired them with a reckless courage. Seizing the olive pole, they drove its sharpened end into the Cyclops's eye, while I used my weight from above to twist it home, like a man boring a ship's timber with a drill which his mates below him twirl with a strap they hold at either end, so that it spins continuously. In much the same way we handled our pole with its red-hot point and twisted it in his eye till the blood boiled up round the burning wood. The fiery smoke from the blazing eyeball singed his lids and brow all round, and the very roots of his eye crackled in the heat. I was reminded of the loud hiss that comes from a great axe or adze when a smith plunges it into cold water – to temper it and give strength to the iron. That is how the Cyclops's eye hissed round the olive stake. He gave a dreadful shriek, which echoed round the

rocky walls, and we backed away from him in terror, while he pulled the stake from his eye, streaming with blood. Then he hurled it away from him with frenzied hands and raised a great shout for the other Cyclopes who lived in neighbouring caves along the windy heights.'

Cyclopes were not the only danger Odysseus faced in his voyaging. The Sirens were creatures who lived on an island to which they would lure sailors by their songs. But those who landed never came away: the island was full of their corpses. Odysseus, though, had been told what to expect, and so he took precautionary measures before sailing:

'I took a large round of wax, cut it up small with my sword, and kneaded the pieces with all the strength of my fingers. The wax soon yielded to my vigorous treatment and grew warm, for I had the rays of my Lord the Sun to help me. I took each of my men in turn and plugged their ears with it. They then made me a prisoner on my ship by binding me hand and foot, standing me up by the step of the mast and tying the rope's end to the mast itself . . . We made good progress and had just come within call of the shore when the Sirens became aware that the ship was swiftly bearing down upon them, and broke into their liquid song.

"Draw near," they sang, "illustrious Odysseus, flower of Achaean chivalry, and bring your ship to rest so that you may hear our voices. No seaman ever sailed his black ship past this spot without listening to the sweet tones that flow from our lips, and none that listened has not been delighted and gone on a wiser man. For we know all that the Argives and Trojans suffered on the broad plain of Troy by the will of the gods, and we have foreknowledge of all that is going to happen on this fruitful earth."

The lovely voices came to me across the water, and my heart was filled with such a longing to listen that with nod and frown I signed to my men to set me free. But they swung forward to their oars and rowed ahead, while Perimedes and Eurylochus jumped up, tightened my bonds and added more.'

One of the earliest representations of Homer, on a Greek coin from the fourth century BC.

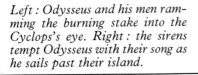

Left: Odysseus and his men ramming the burning stake into the Cyclops's eye. Right: the sirens tempt Odysseus with their song as he sails past their island.

Religion

Besides language and the shared tradition of which Homer is the best example, Greeks also had a religion in common. This was not a clear body of doctrine, with special people charged with its teaching and ritual, and a 'church' of believers, with a definite organization. Instead there was a jumble of myths, ideas and superstitions, none of which *had* to be believed, but some of which tried to make sense of deep and continuing problems of human life – of the insecurity of good fortune, for example, or of the fate (*nemesis*, the Greeks called it) awaiting people who dared to flaunt the rules by which life is run. Myths were a way of coming to grips with the puzzles of life. The practice of religion consisted for the most part of carrying out rituals which would keep the gods in a good mood. We have similar helpful myths but they are related to science rather than the gods: we say that someone's behaviour is 'explained' by an unhappy childhood and this makes us feel we can do something about problems, by, for example, going to a psychiatrist. When this turns out all right, our faith is reinforced. Like us the Greeks had remedies which were based on faith, but on faith in different things from today's, and theirs often seemed to work too.

There were many different sides to Greek religion. It might mean seeking help from mysterious and semi-magical cults, for example. In important cases, oracles could be consulted. The chief oracle was that of Apollo at Delphi, but to many others people made long pilgrimages to get guidance about their destiny. Then there were the gods of each city, living, people thought, in the temples usually to be found on the Acropolis, and served in civic festivals or by sacrifices at household and wayside altars. To these must

The Temple of Athena, built in the fourth century BC *at Delphi, is a late addition to a site which already had many buildings on it, including the famous oracle of Apollo.*

be added the hundreds of very minor gods, demons and powers of nature to whom there were thousands of shrines. From the amount of attention paid to them and the efforts to placate them, it seems that these were the most important aspects of Greek religion.

Finally, sacrifices could also be made to the gods and goddesses of the myths shared by all Hellenes. These gods would often intervene in human life, it was thought, if they were displeased, but probably more attention was given to them in the official state cults than by individuals in their private affairs. These are the gods who appear in Homer. The greatest of them lived, thought the Greeks, on Mount Olympus. Their names – Zeus, Ares, Aphrodite – have become part of the European heritage of myth and legend. The remarkable thing about them is that they are very human. Zeus, king of the gods, is certainly a terrible figure, giving to hurling thunderbolts, but he

is also a well-meaning, often bungling, middle-aged gentleman who is somewhat over-given to chasing girls. Aphrodite, goddess of love and fertility, is also a woman with her own vanities, likes and dislikes. These deities are involved in human affairs too; they do not stand aloof from men. Homer shows Poseidon, god of the sea and of earthquakes, dogging the path of Odysseus with misfortune because of a grudge against him, while the hero's side is taken (and he is helped) by Athena, the virgin goddess of war and wisdom.

Language, a traditional literature, religion: on these grounds the Greeks felt themselves to be one. This did not stop them from having bitter quarrels. But the things which they shared were what they had in mind when they used a word which meant something wider than the mere geographical unity of Greece, yet something just as separate from the outside world: Hellas.

Right: this Greek drinking vessel shows Pluto, god of the underworld, and Persephone banqueting. The Greeks thought of the gods as very much like themselves, and this could be a picture of any well-to-do Greek couple in a relaxed mood. Below: the mythological side of Greek religion appears in this illustration of Athena, springing armed from the head of Zeus, who is clutching a thunderbolt in one hand.

Greeks overseas

No Greek either in Greece or the islands lived more than seventy kilometres from the sea. This must have been a help in making the idea of sea-travel a little less frightening than to inland peoples. It made it easier to look farther afield for places to settle when, as seems to have happened in the eighth century BC, a growing population began to press hard on available space. In societies which had to raise their own food, this meant that people had to seek land elsewhere. This was the main force behind a great movement of colonization, which eventually spread Greek cities even farther over the Mediterranean and the Aegean than the Dorian invasions had done.

There may have been another factor at work too. After the crumbling of the Mycenaean trading connexions, much of the business of the eastern Mediterranean had passed into the hands of the Phoenician cities of the Levant. The Phoenicians had a trade-route along the North African coast which went as far as Cadiz (which they founded) in south Spain. This may have encouraged Greeks to look to the west for places to which they could export their surplus population. They were probably not seeking to compete in trade at this time; what they wanted was land. Nor were they seeking to conquer other cities, though they were prepared to fight the local farmers and graziers, if there were any. What a Greek city would be looking for was a site where a new daughter-city could be set up to become independent of the mother-city from which the colonists had set out; it would become self-sufficient and autonomous as she was.

The first Greek settlement in the west was set up on the bay of Naples in about 750 BC by an expedition sent out by the two cities of Chalkis and Eretria. In the next century or so Greek cities appeared on almost every cultivable coastal plain in Sicily and southern Italy,

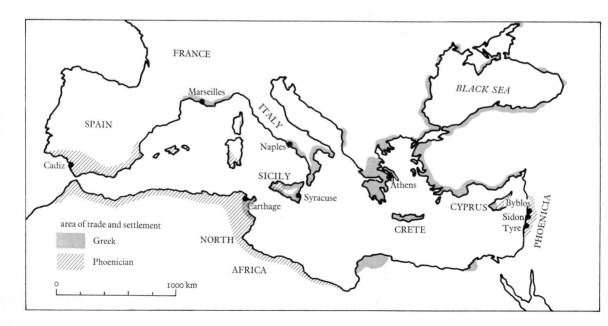

FRANCE

BLACK SEA

Marseilles

ITALY

SPAIN

Naples

Cadiz

SICILY

Syracuse

Athens

Carthage

CYPRUS

Byblos

Sidon

CRETE

Tyre

PHOENICIA

area of trade and settlement

Greek

Phoenician

NORTH

AFRICA

0   1000 km

Left: one of the few pieces of pottery to survive from Sparta, this sixth-century cup shows a busy trading scene on the North African coast.

Below: a Greek coin, minted in Syracuse in 497 BC, with the head of the city's divine patroness on one side of it.

and eventually in some places on the North African and French coasts too. (This was how Marseilles was founded.) The greatest of the new cities was Syracuse, in Sicily; later, in what are called 'classical' times (roughly 500–350 BC), Syracuse and Athens were the only Greek cities with more than 100,000 inhabitants. It was not long, though, before several of the western settlements actually outstripped in population and wealth the cities which had founded them.

As good sites in Sicily and Italy were snapped up, some Greeks turned to the east. They began to follow up the old Ionian expansion of Dorian times. But there was a problem in the Levant; the Phoenicians might be mastered, but the Assyrians were a different proposition. No Greek city could take on such a great power single-handed. Cities looking for sites for new settlements therefore turned north again. Some Greeks settled on peninsulas in the northern Aegean, pushing out or

enslaving the surviving Pelasgoi, but others sailed through the Dardanelles and into the Black Sea. This led, roughly a century after the first, to a second wave of colonizing from about 650 BC which in the end founded a chain of Greek cities all round the Black Sea. These were often more interested in trade than the cities in the west. This was some compensation for the climate in the northern Euxine (as the Greeks called the Black Sea), which was in winter very unattractive to Greeks brought up to life in the outdoors. The new business they gave rise to in the Aegean was important in enriching the Greek cities.

Colonists were not the only Greeks to go abroad. In the sixth century BC there were Greek mercenaries in foreign armies (notably in Egypt), Greek craftsmen at work in Persia, Greek merchants trading everywhere. The whole Mediterranean world was by then much more tied together than it had been in the Dark Ages.

Great powers

Many of the foreigners with whom the Greeks had dealings, especially after the two great surges of expansion, must have been by any test (and not only in the special Greek sense of the word) barbarians. The Scythians with whom the Black Sea Greek cities traded, for example, were truly uncivilized. The fierce Thracian mountaineers were a rough lot too. But elsewhere lands and peoples with more developed societies confronted the Greeks and had to be taken into account by them.

The Near East

The Assyrian empire was at the height of its power in the middle of the seventh century BC, but it did not long survive. For about a hundred years there was a succession of wars in western Asia, during which Assyria crumbled under the attacks of the Medes (a people from Iran), her Babylonian subjects broke away, and a new Mesopotamian empire was set up by a great conqueror of whom we read in the Jewish Bible, Nebuchadnezzar. He ruled in great state and the 'Hanging Gardens' or terraces of Babylon, his capital, were numbered by the ancients among the Seven Wonders of the World. His lands stretched from Egypt across Palestine and Syria to the farther borders of Mesopotamia. It was Nebuchadnezzar who carried off the Jewish people from Palestine in 587 BC, after destroying Jerusalem and the Temple, and imposed on them the Exile, which was to be so important an episode in their national history. Nevertheless this was the last great empire to be based on Mesopotamia and the old traditions which went back to Sumer. In 539 BC a new conqueror from farther east overthrew it. This was Cyrus, the ruler of Persia.

Persia

The story of Persia goes back well before 1000 BC, when the Indo-European migrations pushed a group of peoples from the north·into the high plateau which is the heart of modern Iran. (The name was not used until much later, but 'Iran' is really the same word as 'Aryan'.) Two of these tribes, the Medes and the Persians, were especially successful; the Medes stayed in the north, the Persians went south, to the Gulf coast. It was Cyrus, a Persian king, who first united them, by overcoming the last independent king of the Medes, before going on to conquests which assembled the largest empire the world had yet seen. It was less centralized than the Assyrian empire, more tolerant of the religions of its subjects and sheltered a civilization which had many beautiful things about it. Persia was also always inclined to expand westwards and its appearance opens a period of a thousand years or so during which, with only one major interruption, there was always to be a great power based on the Iranian highlands. Once properly tapped, the resources of this area were likely to make it a formidable military base. Iran was rich in metals, especially iron, and the high pastures sheltered huge reserves of horses and cavalrymen. The rulers who controlled such resources were bound to have an influence on the destinies of Mediterranean peoples.

Cyrus' son added Egypt to the empire, but his successor, Darius (522–486 BC), was the greatest of the kings of what is called Achaemenid Persia (after the family to which Cyrus belonged). Under him the eastern boundaries of the Persian empire were extended as far as the Indus, and in the west he tried, unsuccessfully, to conquer Greece in 490 BC. In his inscriptions he called himself 'Great King, King

The 'Tripylon' staircase at Persepolis, with relief carvings of dignitaries bearing offerings to Darius.

The ruins of Persepolis. The city was destroyed by Alexander the Great in 330 BC.

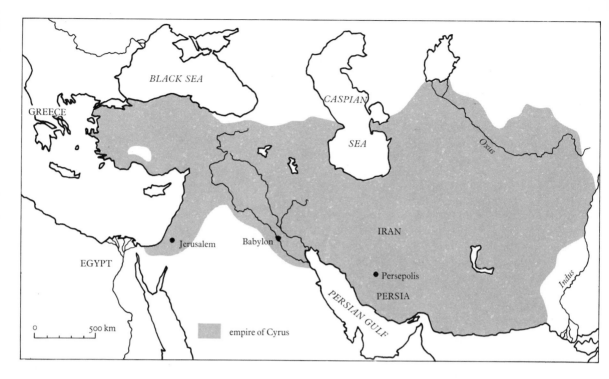

BLACK SEA

CASPIAN

GREECE

SEA

Oxus

IRAN

Jerusalem

Babylon

EGYPT

Persepolis

PERSIA

PERSIAN GULF

Indus

0   500 km

empire of Cyrus

of Kings', an old Achaemenid title still borne by the former Shah of Iran. Decentralization under provincial overlords called 'satraps', and better roads (government messages could travel nearly 300 kilometres a day along the best ones) made the empire easier to govern. At Persepolis Darius began to build a great new capital for it, though he died before it was complete. Its ruins show how open Persia was to outside influences, for much of the work was done by Ionian sculptors and stone-cutters, and the details show Greek styles.

This is an important sign. As no previous empire had done, the Persian empire took in all sorts of traditions from the whole area which it administered. The Persian contribution to this, too, was a large one, notably in religion. Although tolerant of other cults, the state's religion was a refined form of an old Indo-European cult of sacrifice and fire. It was named after Zoroaster, a teacher of whom we do not know very much, but who seems to have encouraged his followers to see the world as an eternal struggle between a good god of light (Ahwa Mazda) and an evil spirit of darkness. These ideas are to be found (with many others) in the sacred book of Zoroastrianism, the *Avesta* (or *Zend-Avesta*), a collection of texts which is all that remains of a much bigger mass of teaching, prayers and hymns. It is about as long as the *Iliad* and *Odyssey* together and is still used as the prayer-book of the Par-

The Achaemenids after Cyrus II

559–30 BC	Cyrus II
530–22	Cambyses II
522–486	Darius I
486–65	Xerxes I
465–24	Artaxerxes I
424–3	Xerxes II
423–404	Darius II
404–359	Artaxerxes II
338–6	Arses
336–30	Darius III

sees of India (their name is derived from the same word as 'Persia'). Many other ideas of Zoroastrianism – the angels which figure in later Christianity, for example, and the idea of a hell awaiting the wicked – were spread throughout the Near East by the Persian supremacy. They were to influence first Judaism and then Christianity, and there are still Zoroastrian communities in Iran today.

Egypt

After the New Kingdom Egypt had fallen on bad times and there is not much to say about it except that it was often ruled by foreigners. At one time, in the eighth century BC, a dynasty of Nubians from the south had set themselves up as pharaohs; they had in their turn been overthrown by the Assyrians. Then followed another brief period of independence before the once great state became first the possession of Nebuchadnezzar and finally a Persian province. This did not close it off from the outside world, though. There are plenty of signs of continuing contact with the Greeks, who, besides finding Egypt a good trading partner, seem to have been fascinated by the many mysterious things they encountered there, from its curious religion and preoccupation with death to its incomprehensible hieroglyph.

The West

The most important power in the West of which the Greeks had to take notice during the first wave of colonization was the city of Carthage. It was later to be destroyed with all its records, and so it remains a city-state of which we do not know very much (though one fact which sticks out is that the Carthaginians had the gruesome habit of sacrificing children to their gods). It was founded somewhere about 800 BC by the Phoenicians and eventually grew to be greater in power and wealth than old Phoenician cities such as Tyre and Sidon. Carthage was later to become a threat to the Greeks of Sicily and southern Italy. In the long run, though, the real danger to the western Greek cities came from farther north, from what was only a cluster of shepherds' huts when Greek colonization was in full swing. This was the future Rome.

The figure on this Persian gold plaque of the fourth century BC or thereabouts is carrying a bundle of rods, which were used as part of Zoroastrian ritual. Today there are less than 100,000 Zoroastrians, some in Iran but most in Bombay, India, where the photograph below was taken. The children are being given a sacred shirt and belt to initiate them into the creed.

The Etruscans and early Rome

The impact of Rome on history and the eagerness of the Romans themselves to invent stirring and fabulous tales about their origin make it very hard to picture the tiny scale on which their story actually began. Traditionally Rome is the city of Seven Hills. Archaeologists disagree about whether the date should be nearer 1000 or 800 BC, but a couple of hut-clusters on the tops of two of the hills, inhabited by graziers who had come there from the neighbouring highlands, were the beginning of settlement. The pasture would have been better there than farther inland, the two sites were easily defensible, and there was a convenient crossing of the River Tiber at that point – the lowest practicable one, in fact, before the sea.

These first Romans were Italians, though not in the modern sense of that word. They belonged to an Indo-European group of peoples which had spread over the whole peninsula in about 1500 BC. Though its site must always have made Rome a key-point in communications, these tiny settlements might never have come to anything had it not been for the arrival shortly before 600 BC of large numbers of the people now called Etruscans. They are in some ways still very mysterious. It seems most likely that they first came by sea from the Balkans in the tenth century, though they may have been joined later by more immigrants, this time from Asia Minor about 700 BC. Certainly, by the time they moved onto the Roman site, the Etruscans were already a mixed people, with knowledge of skills and cultures foreign to Italy. Since arriving in the peninsula, they had become

Above: an Etruscan stone head, made before 500 BC.
Left: the figure of a woman on an Etruscan sarcophagus (a large container for a corpse), about 300 BC.

A delicately worked bronze statuette of an Etruscan warrior.

skilled metal-workers and they exploited the rich iron ore deposits of Elba as well as those on the mainland.

Much remains unknown about the way they ran their affairs, but it looks as if they lived in a loose federation of cities ruled by kings. Etruria, the area they dominated, was at one time very large, running from the River Po in the north down to the coastal plain south of the Tiber. They were literate and had adopted the Greek alphabet – perhaps from Greek cities like Cumae in the south – but many of their inscriptions have not yet been understood.

Since the Etruscans were city-dwellers (one of their cities, Caere, had about 25,000 inhabitants in 600 BC, many Greeks among them), their arrival in large numbers at Rome must have transformed the place. The Romans later stressed the idea of the city and the citizen (they dated their calendar *ab urbe condita* – 'from the founding of the city' – later wrongly put at 753 BC in the Christian calendar) but this was far from being all that they owed to the Etruscans. From them they adopted the Greek myth that Aeneas, a Trojan hero mentioned in the *Iliad*, had escaped the overthrow of Troy and had sailed west to found Rome. It was through the Etruscans too that the

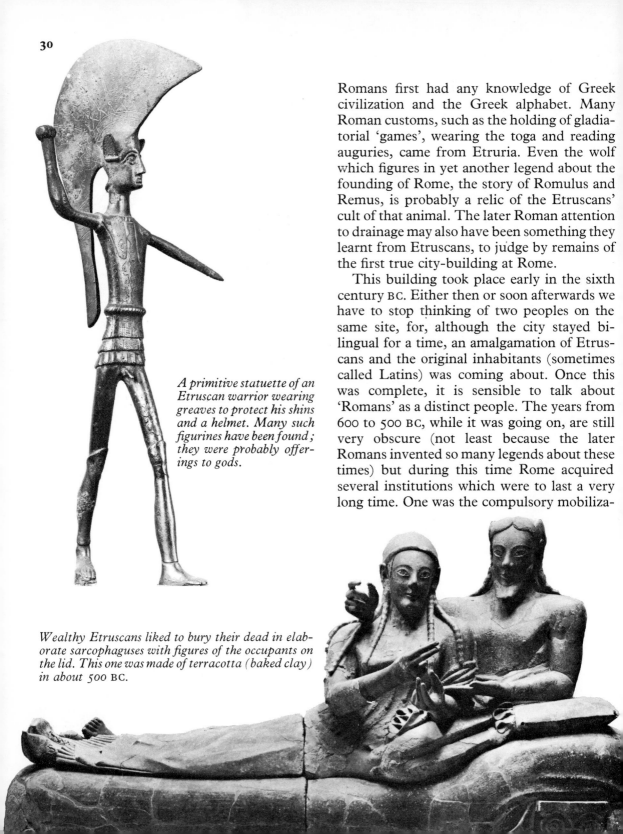

A primitive statuette of an Etruscan warrior wearing greaves to protect his shins and a helmet. Many such figurines have been found; they were probably offerings to gods.

Wealthy Etruscans liked to bury their dead in elaborate sarcophaguses with figures of the occupants on the lid. This one was made of terracotta (baked clay) in about 500 BC.

Romans first had any knowledge of Greek civilization and the Greek alphabet. Many Roman customs, such as the holding of gladiatorial 'games', wearing the toga and reading auguries, came from Etruria. Even the wolf which figures in yet another legend about the founding of Rome, the story of Romulus and Remus, is probably a relic of the Etruscans' cult of that animal. The later Roman attention to drainage may also have been something they learnt from Etruscans, to judge by remains of the first true city-building at Rome.

This building took place early in the sixth century BC. Either then or soon afterwards we have to stop thinking of two peoples on the same site, for, although the city stayed bilingual for a time, an amalgamation of Etruscans and the original inhabitants (sometimes called Latins) was coming about. Once this was complete, it is sensible to talk about 'Romans' as a distinct people. The years from 600 to 500 BC, while it was going on, are still very obscure (not least because the later Romans invented so many legends about these times) but during this time Rome acquired several institutions which were to last a very long time. One was the compulsory mobiliza-

Wrestlers in a wall painting in an Etruscan tomb.

tion of the citizens for military service; military duties went with civil rights in early Rome. Another was the restriction of effective government to 'patricians' or nobles; these took their name from their position as *patres*, or heads of families. The basic Roman religious beliefs took shape before 500 BC too.

When finally the last Etruscan king was expelled (traditionally in 510 BC, though this is probably three or four years out), Rome had really emerged from the Etruscan chrysalis. The Etruscans were by then having a bad time elsewhere. They were turned out of Campania by the Greeks, who also took Elba from them. For a time the new Roman republic continued to have friendly relations with the near-by Etruscan cities, since she had to face grave threats from other neighbours and the communications she controlled mattered to Etruscan trade. But the fifth century BC saw the beginning of a long period of war with the Etruscan cities too. At roughly the same time the last traces of Etruscan presence at Rome – inscriptions and trade-goods, for instance – cease. Rome had by then become truly independent, though struggling with grave weaknesses and far from the world power she was to become.

A bronze statuette, from the fourth century BC, of an Etruscan ploughman with his team of oxen. Even recently the peasantry have made up the bulk of the Italian population, and this might have been a typical sight in rural Tuscany long after Etruscan times.

The *polis*

Homer's poems talk about kings, and a few Greek cities went on calling some of their officials kings in later times, but already, once we have good historical records, we find they were usually governed by 'aristocrats' – a Greek word meaning the 'best people'. Aristocrats were landowners rich enough to buy the expensive arms, armour and horses which made them leaders in war. They ruled over other Greeks who were, in the main, farmers; in most of the Greek world this was always how most free men got their living.

This very simple society had begun to change and grow more complicated at an early date, certainly by 600 BC. Often, for example, foreigners (most of them other Hellenes) who were craftsmen and traders appeared and provided services; they were called 'metics' and were not given the same rights as the native-born inhabitants of a city. Such changes seem to have owed much to the upsurge in trade which followed the second wave of colonization. There was more money about and men grew richer. One sign of what was happening was that the use of metal currency became common in the Greek world. People and communities began to specialize in different kinds of business too. Gradually the old, simple economic arrangements of a society where only big and small landowners mattered became more complicated. Some states began to specialize in certain manufactures. Athens, for example, did so in pottery.

As they grew wealthier, more men could buy land. They could also afford arms and armour, and in the seventh century BC there appeared a new sort of warrior – the 'hoplites'. These were infantry, wearing bronze helmets and body-armour, carrying shields and spears. With them Greek warfare suddenly changed. Earlier fighting was very much a matter of single combat between the few who could afford weapons and armour, which made them much more powerful than most of those who followed them to battle. Now battles began to be won by disciplined masses of hoplites. They kept careful formation, each man being protected on his right-hand side by the shield of his neighbour. On the little valley-floors which were the usual place for Greek battle (since the aim was normally to destroy or defend the crops grown there) a good hoplite formation was almost invulnerable if it charged as a mass and kept its ranks unbroken.

As more men shared military experience, and as discipline and drill mattered more in winning battles, power began to slip from the old aristocracies, because they ceased to be the only people controlling armed force. This was a very remarkable and important change, for it gave rise to the invention of politics.

We take the word 'politics' for granted and often do not bother to think very much about what we mean by it. A rough definition might be this: 'a way of running public affairs by making decisions about them after discussing in public different courses of action'. This may sound somewhat up in the air. Obviously the amount of discussion you have can vary enormously. Nonetheless there is a big difference between public business carried out after discussion and that resting on the arbitrary will of a despot, as the Greeks well knew from looking at Persia or Egypt.

The first 'citizens' in the Greek states – those who were entitled to take part in public affairs – were those who could afford to take their place in the hoplite ranks and fight to defend their heritage. Many fierce struggles must have taken place about which we now know very little, but, little by little, new men everywhere were winning admission to citizen-

The original Acropolis of Athens was devastated by the Persians in 480 BC. After the war Pericles organized the construction of completely new buildings, whose beauty and grandeur can still be seen in their ruins.

A group of typical Athenian citizens (left) and, in contrast, a Spartan hoplite dressed for battle (right).

ship in the sixth century BC. Government by aristocrats gave way to government by popular strong men – 'tyrants', the Greeks called them – but these in their turn eventually gave way almost everywhere to governments with a broader base. Some cities were ruled by the well-off (the 'oligarchies'), others by the main body of free men (the 'democracies'). But what tended to happen almost everywhere was that rule by hereditary leaders was replaced by something much more widely based.

'Oligarchy' and 'democracy' are Greek words we still use. So, in their origins, are 'politics' and 'political'. Both came from the Greek word for a state or independent city: *polis*. This is a difficult word to translate. It meant more than just a place; in fact the Greeks did not speak of 'Athens' doing this, or 'Thebes' doing that, but of what was done by 'the Athenians' and 'the Thebans'. *Polis* is usually translated 'city-state', for want of a better term, but in some ways it was not much like a city and it was certainly much more than we often mean nowadays by 'state'. It was a community of people. The *polis* community did not include everyone who lived in the city and surrounding countryside – which is what it would seem to be on the map – but was only the citizens: those who had to take their place in the hoplite ranks in war and had a say, however small, in their common affairs. Slaves, foreigners and women could not be citizens. It was more like belonging to a tribe than our modern notion of citizenship.

For a long time most examples of the *polis* were fairly small. Only an unusual *polis* had 20,000 citizens. Most citizen-bodies could therefore make all their members feel much more personally involved in public life than do the citizens of a modern state. They took part as a body in things which we have hived off to private organizations like clubs and churches.

Part of a 'kleroterion', a device used for selecting jurors. The names of potential jurors were placed in the slots, and whole rows of jurors were arbitrarily either selected for service or sent away.

Juror's ballots: if the defendant was to be acquitted, those with solid hubs were put into the ballot-box, while a hollow hub, like the middle one, meant condemnation.

A fifth-century 'ostrakon', which was a ballot with the name scratched on it of the person to be voted out of power or even into exile. The name on this ticket is 'Aristeides'.

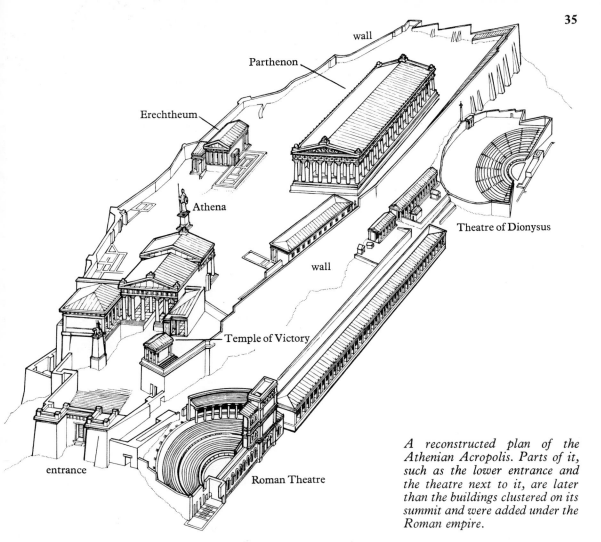

wall

Parthenon

Erechtheum

Athena

Theatre of Dionysus

wall

Temple of Victory

entrance

Roman Theatre

A reconstructed plan of the Athenian Acropolis. Parts of it, such as the lower entrance and the theatre next to it, are later than the buildings clustered on its summit and were added under the Roman empire.

Religion was a matter of civic gods; Athena might be worshipped elsewhere, but at Athens she was *the* deity, the special guardian of the city, with festivals in which all citizens joined. These religious occasions were often also mingled with other activities – athletics and games, for example, or theatrical performances. And there was always the assembly of all the citizens, where a Greek would get to know how his friends, enemies and acquaintances felt on questions that affected them all.

All these things made life in the *polis* an intense, demanding business, but also a more exciting one than that of a modern state. It is not surprising, then, that Greeks came to think that the *polis* gave men the chance to be themselves – to release all the potential of their human nature – in a way no other kind of human organization did. You could, they thought, be civilized in a *polis* as you could not be elsewhere. Man, said one Greek philosopher, was a creature made by nature to live in a *polis*. The Greeks had another word which tells us a lot about the way they thought of their public life. It was the word they applied to someone who, as it were, 'dropped out' and would not take part in or concern himself with public affairs: 'idiot'.

The Persian wars

The Etruscans sometimes pressed hard on the western Greeks of Italy in the sixth century BC, and the Carthaginians were always a threat to those in Sicily. Still, these enemies were held off: at the beginning of the fifth century it was the eastern Greeks who were having the rougher time at the hands of their neighbours.

This was nothing new. The Ionian cities had always been open to blackmail or invasion by Asian powers and at the beginning of the fifth century it looked as if mainland Greece too was threatened by continuing Persian expansion. Greeks and Persians came more and more into contact in Asia Minor as the Persians conquered the non-Greek kingdoms there. They even pushed across the Dardanelles and occupied cities on the Thracian coast. Finally the Greeks of Ionia revolted against the demands made on them; some of them were especially annoyed when the Persians interfered in their internal affairs – for example, by supporting tyrants against their subjects. With some of the mainland cities behind them, Ionians were for a time successful. But eventually they were overcome. The Persians then decided to punish mainland Greece for its support of the revolt.

One naval attack failed, but another Persian fleet set out in 490 BC. The army it carried was beaten by the Athenians at Marathon, where the discipline of the hoplites showed that even the great Persian army was not invincible. But the Persians came back ten years later, in 480 BC. This time they moved by land down the coast after a great bridge of boats had been built at the Dardanelles for their army to cross to Europe. The Persian fleet covered its flank as it moved slowly forward. This time the Spartans took the lead in the Greek defence. The first great combat was at the pass of Thermopylae, where Leonidas, the Spartan

The pass at Thermopylae.

Opposite: a Greek vase from the sixth century BC shows a warrior getting ready for battle, while his wife or a servant holds his spear and shield.

Right: a relief, made in the fifth century BC, showing Greek soldiers in battle. Their lack of body armour could be compensated for by the large shields they carried.

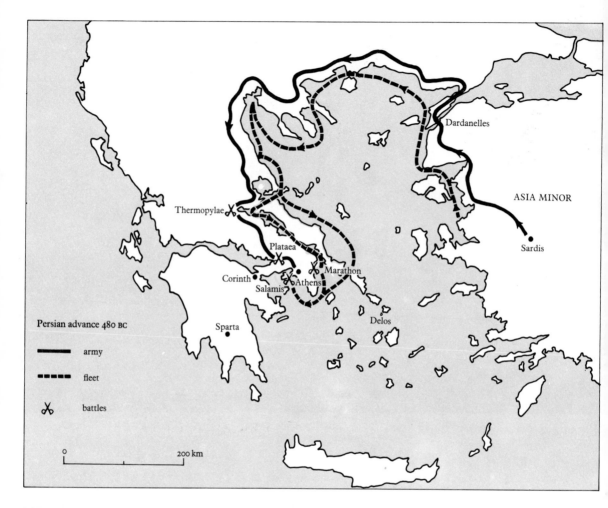

Persian advance 480 BC

————— army

▪ ▪ ▪ ▪ ▪ fleet

✂ battles

0   200 km

king, and 300 soldiers were overwhelmed but left an imperishable legend of heroism to the the future. The Persians pressed on. Attica had to be given up to them, Athens was taken and destroyed and the Greeks fell back on Corinth, massing their fleet in the bay of Salamis.

By now it was autumn. Perhaps because he feared the onset of winter – which can be harsh in Greece – the Persian king decided to make an end of it and attacked the Greek fleet. But in the narrow waters of Salamis he lost the advantage of numbers. The Greeks shattered his fleet, and, without its support and supply, the Persian army had to retreat. In the next year (479 BC) it was defeated at Plataea and on the same day the Greeks won another great victory at Mycale, on the Asian coast, where another Persian fleet was burned.

Though the war dragged on for years, this was really the end of the Persian threat and it opened the greatest age of Greek history. The Ionian cities were now liberated, under the leadership of the Athenians and, so far as politics went, the following decades were marked by growing Athenian power. This was accompanied by growing fear of Athens elsewhere, especially at Sparta.

Sparta and Athens show how big the contrast might be between one *polis* and another. Sparta was ruled by a large aristocracy (about 5000, according to fifth-century writers) in a very austere, somewhat puritanical way. Luxury was forbidden; Spartans were not supposed to own gold or silver. Sparta played little part in the colonizing movement and remained wholly agricultural, conquering more land from its neighbours as required. Her citizens were not rich but held down a large population of serfs – called 'helots' – and prided themselves on their military achievements. In Sparta the hoplite tradition was especially vigorous.

By contrast, fifth-century Athens, rebuilt and restored to prosperity after the disaster of 480 BC, was a great commercial city. Of all the Greek states, her government was the most democratic, all decisions being taken by the general assembly of the citizens (not that they would all be able to be present, or that they were a majority of the inhabitants). In the aftermath of the Persian wars the Athenians made something like a bid for Hellenic leadership based on their naval power. A league was formed to support a common fleet to fight the Persians (the Spartans did not join). Its members at first contributed ships, then they began simply to pay money to the Athenians to build and man them. When members refused to pay up, thinking the Persian danger now remote, the Athenians forced them to do so. Even after peace was made the Delian League (as it was called because its headquarters was at first the island of Delos) went on. At its height, 150 states were paying tribute to Athens.

Top dogs are rarely popular, but the Athenians won a fair amount of support and admiration in the league. This was because they tended to interfere with the internal affairs of other cities and back up democratic regimes where they existed. The richer citizens of other cities did not like this – after all, it was they who paid the taxes which went into the tribute to Athens. On the other hand, the poor majority, who were supported by the Athenians (often by force), did not mind taxing their rich fellow-citizens, nor, it seems, that the money was increasingly spent not on the Athenian navy but on beautifying Athens with splendid buildings and monuments.

As the fifth century went on, the Greek world began to look more and more divided. On the one side were many democratic states looking to Athens for leadership. The Athenians associated democracy with the anti-Persian struggle and their own naval supremacy (somewhat in the way many nineteenth-century Englishmen thought that the spread of civilization and constitutional government was inseparable from the naval supremacy which guaranteed their empire). On the other side were the more oligarchic and aristocratic states anxious to avoid trouble with the Persians and fearing the further extension of Athenian power.

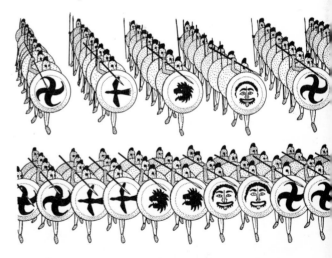

Much of the Greeks' success in battle was owed to the fact that at an early date they introduced a disciplined formation, which was to be further developed in the Macedonian phalanx (see page 60). Regular formation was much easier to maintain when a new large shield was introduced. It covered the soldier's torso when in open order and helped protect his neighbour's unguarded side in close order.

How the Greeks lived

Civilization has been in existence for just over five thousand years; by 500 BC its story is more than half told. Huge changes had by then already taken place in the way men thought about the world since civilization had first begun in Sumer, and the Greeks of that time are fewer centuries away from us than they were from the first civilized men. Yet some things had not changed very much. For example, there would have been no very obvious change in the way most people got their living, for agriculture was still laborious and pretty primitive. Even today, we sometimes forget, most people in the world are peasants, and this was certainly true in Hellas. It took only a few hundred potters, for example, to keep going the big export trade in pottery from Athens. The largest shield factory in the city was thought enormous because 120 people worked in it. There were relatively few smiths, stone-cutters, armourers, jewellers and other specialists; agriculture was the backbone of the economy, as it was in every country in the world until the nineteenth century and still is today in a great many.

This agriculture had not much changed since the arrival of the basic skills from Asia. Greek soil is not usually rich and the range and quality of crops available remained poor throughout classical times. Plots were very small – even a rich man could have as little as 20–30 hectares of mixed cornfields and vine-yards according to one classification by wealth of Athenian citizens early in the sixth century. Reliance on a smallholding agriculture meant that Greek society was not very wealthy in our terms; life was hard and simple for most Greeks. When we look at the great ruins of Hellas – at the Parthenon at Athens, for example, or the many Greek temples which survive more or less complete – we are in danger of getting a false impression of Greek life. These were, after all, public buildings, paid for by collective resources. Most Greeks would have lived in pretty humble little houses, would have eaten fairly plain food and would not have had servants or slaves.

This would have been true of the class which mattered most in the *polis* – the citizenry. The great dividing line was not wealth, nor that between free and unfree, but between those who were citizens and those who were

A Greek vase-painter has shown himself or a fellow craftsman at work.

A terracotta figure of a Greek sawing wood. The saw he is using looks similar in design to the bow saw still used today.

Opposite : work was hard for the Greek ploughman in the sixth century BC. *After driving his plough through the earth, he had to set to work with a pick to loosen the soil even more.*

This sixth-century vase shows a diver about to enter the sea from a boat. He is probably earning his living by gathering sponges or shellfish.

not. The overall tendency for a very long time was for estates to be sub-divided again and again at inheritance, and most citizens and free peasants who were not citizens would have been smallholders on our reckoning. Some states faced grave problems from the growing impoverishment of their peasants. Some free men, of course, were quite landless. Such were the 'thetes', who worked for hire for others, and there seemed to be more of them as time passed. The 'metics', whose numbers grew rapidly in states where trade flourished, were another important group of freemen who were not citizens.

It has been estimated that about forty per cent of the male population of fifth-century Athens were non-citizens of one sort and another, but Athens was a very unusual place in its dependence on trade and manufactures. Athens also had proportionately more really wealthy men than in earlier times. Old, aristocratic families provided some of them – those who lived on incomes from their estates – and among these there was a prejudice against earning money by entering a profession or by trade. But the ranks of the wealthy were also added to by rich merchants.

The only other important group of inhabitants of the *polis* with a special legal position were the slaves. In archaic times the losers in wars were sometimes enslaved, though the men were usually killed and only the women, who could be put to work at domestic drudgery, were likely to be spared. Apart from such conquests, slaves were either born to slavery, condemned to it by a court, or bought in one of the great markets of Asia Minor. A feeling grew up in the fifth and fourth centuries BC that there was something wrong and unnatural about Greeks having Greeks as slaves; but there were Greek slaves all the same.

There were fewer slaves, it seems, in Greece than in the great oriental empires or in later Roman times, and this has much to do with the shape of Greek agriculture. Small farmers could just about rub along getting a living for themselves and their families. They could afford neither to buy a slave, nor to feed him, because he could not do enough to earn his keep. There were no great estates relying on slave-labour, and more slaves were to be found in the towns than in the country. In the towns they worked at all kinds of tasks as servants and craftsmen. (One who became famous was Aesop, the story-teller.) In the fifth century about a quarter of the population of Athens seem to have been slaves, though no section of the economy absolutely depended on their labour, except the silver-mines owned by the state. Slaves who were not in full-time personal service were hired out in gangs and paid like free labourers; they often worked alongside free men on the same tasks. The slave had to give his master a part of his wages, but his

One of a servant's less pleasant duties: tending a reveller who is obviously about to regret his party activities.

position was in many ways not very different from that of a poor free labourer.

Slaves could be freed and could also buy their freedom, though this does not seem to have happened very often. However, their lot was not likely to be much improved by being free if they were already working for wages. We do not hear much of slave revolts (the Spartan helots, or serfs, were a different matter), but this does not tell us much about how slaves were treated. Probably most domestic slaves were not treated too badly, but we know that in the silver-mines of Attica they had to endure very harsh conditions, although this would have been less striking to ancient Greeks than it is to us. Everyone, after all, had a hard life in those days by modern standards. What was distinctive about the slave was that another man had absolute power over him.

Free women also had no rights of citizenship. Some evidence suggests that Greek women led pretty cramped and sheltered lives in other ways too, but there were big differences between different states' customs. Most Greeks seem to have thought that Spartan girls were given too much freedom (and certainly deplored the very brief gym-slips in which they exercised together with the boys). The women of a wealthy household in Athens, on the other hand, lived in separate quarters, locked off at night from the rest. In case this should suggest the seclusion of the eastern harem, we should remember that its purpose was probably to stop men getting at the servant-girls – if they were pregnant or had young children with them, they would be less use as servants and meant more mouths to feed. Still, we also know that respectable married women were likely to be veiled when they went out, did not leave the house alone and were not expected to talk to anyone they met. The Greeks liked parties – their pottery shows that – but there seems to have been nothing of the easy atmosphere of the mixed gatherings of Egyptian ladies and gentlemen we see in tomb-paintings; Greek men might never meet their friends' womenfolk. If they did meet a woman at a party, she was almost certainly a professional entertainer called a 'hetaira'. They were somewhat like Geisha girls in Japan – more than mere prostitutes, with skills in singing, conversation and dancing, but by no means respectable, since their charms were for sale. Some were famous and their names have come down to us.

There was virtually no activity outside the home open to a Greek lady of good family, in fact. Poor women could work for others, but a lady could not. Nor could any woman become a nurse, actress, scribe or anything similar because such female professions did not exist. At home, though, there was plenty to do.

The Greeks used much less furniture than we do today, but what they had was often of high-quality workmanship. The chest into which this woman is putting her tidily folded cloth is engraved with mythological scenes.

Greek women not only washed the clothes, but made them, probably after weaving the material from thread they had themselves spun. The management of the household was much more complicated and time-consuming than it would be today.

One reason why Athenian women (to take a particular example) had fewer legal rights than men was that Greek society (like virtually every other before our own) respected the interests of the family rather than the individual. Accordingly, since the society was patriarchal, women could not hold property or conduct business and were always the legal wards of their husbands or nearest male relatives. If a daughter was left sole heiress to her father's estate, her nearest male kinsman was entitled and enjoined to claim her in marriage to ensure that the property remained in the family.

It is hard to say anything in general terms about exactly how Greek women were regarded. One problem is that much of our evidence is drawn from literature, but domestic life hardly makes an appearance there. Yet we know that women went to the theatre in Athens; they must have watched and listened to Antigone, Electra, Jocasta, Medea – the great female characters of Greek tragedy – and many other very varied female roles. They can hardly have made sense of them if they were themselves simply empty-headed drudges. On tombstones and vases there are pictures of dead wives taking leave of their families which suggest deep affection; there does not seem to be any evidence suggesting the lack of respect involved in, say, the veiled and confined life of an oil sheikh's wife today. Socrates' wife nagged him; she certainly did not behave subserviently, and many Greek wives must have been like her. All in all, it is best to be cautious about Greek attitudes to women, then. Homer said that 'there is nothing finer than when a man and his wife live together in true union, sharing the same thoughts'; it is worth remembering that this was something every educated Greek must have read.

When small, Greek children were brought up by their mothers but, if the boys were going to go to school (girls never did), they left their mothers' charge at an early age. The education received by a Greek boy of a family which could afford it placed great emphasis on learning by heart – there are tales of learning the whole of Homer in this way – and literature with writing, music and gymnastics made up most of the curriculum. The aim was to produce the 'whole man', to provide a rounded education which would fit someone to take his place in the *polis*, sharing its values and tastes, rather than to train in specialist skills – something Greeks thought best left to slaves. There were no universities until something like one appeared at Athens, in the Academy which Plato founded, but the general standard of literacy – to judge by the Athenian practice of using public notice boards and inscriptions – seems to have been quite high.

A vase-illustration of a child sitting in its potty-chair and holding a rattle. Presumably a child could be safely left untended for some time in this solid construction.

Women at work, collecting water from public fountains.

A Greek lady at her toilet attended by servants. Her hair has not yet been tied back in the style customary for Greek women.

A Greek scent-bottle shaped like a sandalled foot.

The Greek miracle

Although Greeks were deeply attached to their past, they produced quite suddenly – many of them within a single century, between about 480 and 380 BC – a rush of achievements many of which were startlingly novel. Ever since, people have wondered how it happened. Some have called it 'the Greek miracle', so amazing do they find it. Much, though by no means all, of this achievement was Athenian. Not all the Greek thinkers, poets and artists of the fifth century were Athenians – and practically no scientists were – and we may somewhat exaggerate the part played by Athenians because we do not know so much about some other places. Still, fifth-century Greeks themselves often recognized that Athens was in a sense their cultural as well as political leader. As one Athenian statesman, Pericles, put it, their city

was a model for the rest of Greece. (An excerpt from this speech appears on p. 55.)

The central feature of the Greek miracle was its contribution to the development of the powers of the human mind. So intense an effort had never before been made to grapple with the deepest problems of thought and life, and there was not to be another like it for a long time. It was a matter of a longer period than the great classical age itself. Overall, in about four hundred years, Greeks invented politics, philosophy, most of arithmetic and geometry (those are all in origin Greek words) and the notions of art accepted by Europeans almost until our own day. This was a huge step. It makes Greek civilization very different from that of Mesopotamia or Egypt. Much of it depends on the new importance the

Greeks gave to rational, conscious inquiry about the world they lived in. The fact that many of them continued to be superstitious and believe in magic does not offset this. Because of the way they used reason and argument, they gave human beings a better grip on the world they lived in than any earlier people had done. This does not mean that Greek ideas were always right, only that they were built on and tested in better ways than earlier ones.

One example can be found in science. Modern science really begins in sixth-century Ionia, where a number of thinkers began to put forward explanations about the way the universe worked in terms of laws and regularities rather than of gods and demons. The Greek philosopher Democritus even arrived at the idea that all matter was made up of 'atoms' – a theory about two thousand years ahead of its time; it did not catch on. Instead the Greeks were to leave behind the idea that all matter was made up of four 'elements' – earth, water, air and fire – combined in different ways in different substances. This was not so near the truth as the atomic theory, but it made further investigation possible and kept science going roughly until the seventeenth century AD. In much the same way the teaching of Hippocrates (a Greek from Cos who was a pupil of Democritus) was the basis of

medicine until very recent times. There is great difficulty in disentangling his personal writings from those attributed to him, but from what was said about him by others it is clear that he marks the real beginning of the scientific study of health, observing symptoms and the effects of treatments, making sensible recommendations about diet and separating knowledge from superstition. The 'Hippocratic Oath' called after him defines the ethics of doctors to this day.

Even more important contributions to the future were made by Greeks in mathematics. This story again starts outside mainland Greece, at Crotone in southern Italy, where there lived a philosopher called Pythagoras. He was one of the first people to argue deductively – that is, by applying pure argument on logical lines to certain first principles or axioms. This was important not only because of the advances in arithmetic and geometry which followed, but because it helped to make other people think clearly and rigorously about problems that were not mathematical. But Pythagoras is probably best known for the theorem about right-angled triangles, which is named after him, though it is in fact of a later date.

One of the most famous of all Greeks in insisting on the importance of rigorous thought

Opposite : this Greek boy is being taught to recite Homer from the scroll held by his teacher. The lettering on the scroll has been enlarged by the illustrator, and would not normally be so big. The man on the boy's right is the 'pedagogue', a family slave who brought the boy to school and watched his behaviour.

Right : a Greek physician examining a patient. The figure looking on may be Asclepios, the Greek god of medicine.

A Roman mosaic, found in Pompeii, showing Plato teaching in Athens. The Acropolis can be seen in the top right-hand corner.

was the Athenian Socrates. He wrote no books and we know of him only through what other people tell us. Most of what he is thought to have said and taught (and he was one of the greatest teachers who has ever lived) is recorded in a series of 'dialogues' or conversations, set down by his greatest pupil, the philosopher Plato. People have argued a great deal about whether what Socrates is reported by Plato as saying was really what he taught or whether it is what Plato would have wished him to say, but the message is clear enough: the most important thing a man can do, says Socrates, is to try to understand how he can live a good life. What is the good at which man should aim? The only way of finding out about this with certainty, Socrates taught, is to examine carefully arguments about such ideas as good, justice, truth – to scrutinize and question the values men live by, in short.

Socrates also said much else, but the most important thing about his teaching is its general drift and the way he did it rather than the conclusions he arrived at. He seemed to question everything normally taken for granted. In the end he was brought to trial at Athens in 399 BC, charged with denying the gods recognized by the state and corrupting the young with his teaching. He was said to have done this in many ways: by teaching disrespect for the institutions; by mocking democracy and public morality by means of citing passages of Homer in a mischievous way; and by teaching the young to disobey their parents. This may have masked political enmity towards Socrates and his friends, but there was no doubt about the legality of his trial and condemnation. There is, after all, no guarantee that democracy will be more tolerant of unconventional views than any other form of regime. Socrates was therefore ordered to commit suicide and did so. (Interestingly he seems to have thought the state had a perfect right to condemn him, which perhaps tells us something about the loyalty the *polis* could call on from its best citizens.)

Ever since Socrates there have been men willing to shake us out of our complacency by questioning everyday beliefs and bringing us up short when we look at familiar ideas in a new light. He has been accused of exaggerating the power of reason, and of using it only negatively, but to expose error and dispose of intellectual rubbish is a necessary step towards discovering the truth. But, of course, by his questioning of so much that was usually taken for granted, Socrates did not help to hold traditional structures together – and the *polis* rested on unquestioned assumptions in the end, as does every human institution.

Socrates' pupil, Plato, was inspired by him and tried to go further. He thought that reason provided us with the certainty that such concepts as justice, beauty, goodness really existed in a world made up of ideas. He did not mean by this that they existed in the sense that they were in someone's mind (as one might say, 'I have an idea') but that somewhere there was a world of changeless reality beyond the changing material world. This reality, which could be reached by the human soul (which he, like Socrates, distinguished from the body) through the use of reason, was made up of such ideas.

Plato did not think much of the way most people behaved (and very little of the Athenian democrats who condemned Socrates). He believed that most people would never be able to live the good life which the real world of ideal 'forms' would reveal. Nevertheless, his teaching was very important. It kept people thinking about all sorts of problems right down to our own day and, in particular, founded an important tradition of thought called Idealism – the belief that in some way or another there exists a world which is more real than that of material experience, is understandable by reason and is not just a matter of incomprehensible magic.

Plato himself had a great pupil, Aristotle, who came from Thrace. He wrote about so many things – biology, physics, mathematics, logic, literature, psychology, ethics, politics – that he left behind enough for learned men to build on for two thousand years. He laid out the main ways in which people have thought about these subjects almost down to the present day. Aristotle was a less abstract thinker than Plato; he liked to collect and classify facts and ideas so as to make clear the general laws which underlay them. In all (though it is almost impossible to judge such a matter) his influence may have been even greater than Plato's. What is certain is that these two Greek philosophers long dominated the history of rational thought as no other two thinkers have done.

The Greeks also made another great intellectual step forward in the fifth century BC by inventing scientific history. *Istorie* was a Greek word; it meant 'inquiry'. One Greek from Asia Minor, Herodotus, is often called the 'father of history'; he was the first man to inquire about events in time and he did so in the first prose work of art in a European language (*Researches* would be a reasonable translation of the title), a huge account of the interplay of Greece and Persia which came down to the end of the Persian war. It is really a history of the world – Herodotus' world. There are tall stories in it, but it is based on a serious consideration of witnesses and accounts of events. His successor, the Athenian Thucydides, was even more scrupulous in his inquiries in the book he wrote towards the end of the century to explain a great struggle called the Peloponnesian war which had erupted inside the Greek world. He has been admired even more than Herodotus for his attempt to explain 'why' as well as 'how' things happened.

Greek philosophy, science, mathematics and history were all ways in which civilization as the growth of reason and intellectual power was carried forward faster than ever before. The Greeks also made great contributions to the arts, in particular to literature. Among other things they founded the theatre as we know it. Greek drama had its roots in rituals carried out at religious festivals, notably those of Dionysus, god of wine. At these festivals choral songs were recited and in the sixth century speeches by an individual actor were added to this. From these simple beginnings more changes followed until, in the fifth century BC, a great series of tragic plays were

Above: the Greek colony of Paestum, founded during the seventh century BC in Italy, is notable still for its magnificent Doric temples. Above right: part of the Erechtheum, begun in 421 and finished in about 405. It stands on the north side of the Acropolis.

Right: classical orders of Greek architecture 1. Doric 2. Ionic 3. Corinthian. The three styles developed between the seventh and fourth centuries BC, each more ornate than the last.

1   2   3

written which (with Homer) are the peak of Greek literary art. They were performed only on semi-religious occasions, civic festivals of importance to all the citizens, and they often retold familiar stories and legends which had religious and supernatural themes woven into them. In the work of the three great Athenian tragedians, Aeschylus, Sophocles and Euripides, the audience was given a fresh look at old and familiar stories, perhaps to bring out some new point not previously likely to be in their minds, though at the heart of Athenian tragedy always lay an emphasis on the mysterious workings of the laws which govern human life and the sad destinies that lie in wait even for the fortunate.

We know that about three hundred tragedies were performed at Athens in the fifth century, but thirty-three by these three leading tragedians are all that survive. There are also some comedies, for the drama developed in more than one way. Aristophanes was the first great comic writer for the stage. From his plays we can see that by his time comedy was turning into a means of commenting on public life – he made fun of Socrates, for example, and wrote the first play about female emancipation (like most authors who took up the theme in the next couple of thousand years, he poked fun at it).

Much Greek architecture and sculpture was to survive to provide models for the future to admire, but we have lost much of what the Greeks would have seen, simply because stone and marble last well whereas paint, wood and fabrics do not. The beautiful ruins on the Acropolis in Athens would have looked much more garish when they were cluttered up with little shrines and when their statues and friezes were painted in bright colours; that is how Greeks would have seen them.

In their architecture, the Greeks borrowed from Asia – the column, for example, which probably came from Egypt, was one such inspiration – though they later evolved a style which was all their own. Their first ideas for statues also probably came from the east, but again the Greeks took them so far as to develop something truly original. Their greatest achievements were in representing the human form; gradually the stiff, ritualistic stances of early statues gave way to natural, easy poses. They seem to have delighted in showing just how splendid a thing the human being could be in both mind and body. The peak of this achievement came in the middle of the fourth century BC with the work of the Athenian Praxiteles.

Although this figure from the sixth century BC (left) is standing in a stiff, formal pose, the beginnings of a more natural and realistic style can be seen in the soft folds of her dress. By the time the Venus de Milo was sculpted (probably towards the end of the fourth century BC) this development is even more marked.

The Greek theatre

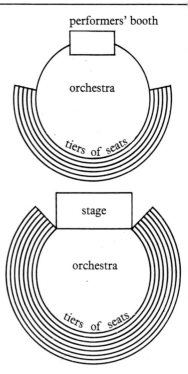

The theatre on the Acropolis of Pergamum in Turkey. It was built in the third century BC, but the Romans made additions to it later.

Europe's first theatres developed from an old festival in honour of Dionysus. At first, people stood in a circle to watch the activities. Then tiers of seats were built in a semi-circle and the artists still performed in the centre, in what was called the orchestra. Eventually, when individual actors became important in Greek drama, a stage encroached on the orchestra and so we arrive at the basic plan and terminology for the theatre today.

Left: special chairs like this one were used for guests of honour or for the judges of the drama competitions. This survives in a Greek theatre at Priene in Turkey, which could hold about 5000 people and was used as a people's parliament as well as a theatre.

Right : a comedy scene on a wine bowl showing a girl's lover climbing a ladder to her window – an event which has gone on being used as a standby of dramatists right down to today.

Above : a second-century Greek terracotta vessel in the form of a comic actor who is impersonating a slave.

Right : Greek actors often wore masks to hide their own features and present expressions more suitable to the roles they were playing. In this picture from a vase a tragic actor is holding his bearded mask.

The Peloponnesian war

For over a quarter of a century, from 431 to 404 BC, a great struggle raged with only brief interruptions, over the whole Greek world. This was the Peloponnesian war, so named because one side consisted of a league of Peloponnesian states led by Sparta. Athens was their main enemy, but at one time or another almost every Greek state was involved. It was so important and without precedent that Thucydides wrote the first historical monograph to explain why it had happened. Historians ever since have agreed that it may have been a turning point in the history of civilization.

At first sight, the origins of the war do not seem very remarkable. There had been growing irritation over the Athenian ascendancy and Sparta had led the opposition to it in a sort

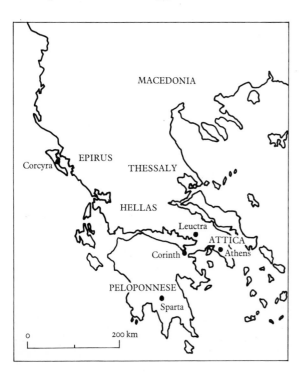

of 'cold war' for about forty years. One outbreak of fighting during this time lasted several years; from time to time, too, Athens and Sparta had each had to take up arms against dissident allies and satellites. Many Athenians seem to have thought another war was bound to come in order to settle whether Athens was to be top dog among the Greek states. The Spartans feared Athenian intentions and had sympathizers wherever there were Greeks who opposed the democratic regimes which Athens seemed to favour. And there was jealousy of Athenian commercial power too, notably on the part of the people of Corinth, another great trading city.

The war started when Corcyra (the modern Corfu), one of the dependencies of Corinth, rebelled and appealed to the Athenians for help. To some at Athens, this seemed an opportunity too good to be missed and, besides, Corcyra was on such an important route to the west (in the days when ships tried to keep in sight of land) that there was a strategic advantage at stake. When the Athenians helped the Corcyrans, the Corinthians complained to the Spartans. Other complaints were made by other cities against Athenian high-handedness, but Pericles, the statesman who dominated Athens, did not encourage his countrymen to make concessions. And so Sparta entered what she called a war of liberation.

The allies of the Athenians and the Spartans were scattered about all over the Greek world, though, broadly speaking, the Athenians had Ionia and the islands on their side, and the Spartans the Peloponnese. The war was therefore really one of sea against land. The Spartans invaded Athenian territory, the Athenians retired behind the walls of the city, allowed their lands to be ravaged and occupied, but fed themselves with the imports their sea-

Democracy in Athens

It was the custom of the Athenians to bury those who had fallen in war at public funerals and Thucydides tells us that they did so on several occasions during the Peloponnesian War. Usually a leading citizen was told to address the crowd at these gatherings and it was in 431 BC, at the funeral of the first of those to die in the war, that Pericles, a leading politician, delivered a speech which has long been regarded as the classic statement of Athenian patriotism and pride in the polis. *These extracts are taken from Thucydides' report of the speech.*

'The constitution we employ does not try to copy the laws of our neighbours. We do not imitate them, but serve rather as an example to them. Because arrangements are not in the hands of the few but of the many, its name is Democracy. In private differences, each man has an equal status in law, but in his public reputation he is preferred according to his ability, with consideration paid not to his class but to his individual merit. In terms of wealth and poverty, if a man can do some service to the state, he is not debarred by obscurity of position. Our public life is regulated with freedom, and in the mutual suspicion of our day to day dealings we are not angry with our neighbour if pleasure is his guide, nor do we inflict on him gloomy looks, which are so unpleasant to see even if they do no actual injury. Our private relationships are thus free from offence, and in our public conduct we abide by the laws mainly from respect, in obedience to those in power at the time and to the laws themselves, especially those of them which were passed to help the wronged and the unwritten laws which bring that dishonour on which we all agree . . .

'We love beauty without luxury and wisdom without softness. We employ our wealth more as an aid to action than as a subject for boasting. We do not think it disgraceful for anyone to be poor; much more disgrace is attached to those who do not try to escape poverty by hard work. It is possible for the same men to care for public and private duties, and in spite of varying occupations to be fully acquainted with politics. We are the only people who consider a man who takes no share of public duties not as lazy but as useless, and the self-same citizens also form judgements and sound opinions about what should be done.

We do not consider argument a hindrance to action, which seems rather to be impeded by no previous discussion. We, too, are unique both in doing the acts of daring and in closely considering what we will attempt; in others ignorance brings boldness, and deliberation fear. Men are rightly held to be greatest of soul who know most soundly the boundaries of pleasure and pain, and for that reason do not shrink from danger. As regards humanity, we are again different from most, for we gain our friends by conferring benefits, not by receiving them. The man who acts thus is more sure to keep alive the gratitude, as if the one on whom he had conferred the benefit owed him a debt of kindness. But the man who should be grateful is the duller friend, knowing that he will be returning the benefit, not as a favour but in settlement of a debt. We do not reckon our personal advantages in conferring these benefits, but have a fearless trust in our freedom.

'. . . With us, each particular person can with ease show himself self-sufficient in most aspects of life and with the most graces. The power which we have won for the city by these manners reveals that this is no verbal boast used for immediate effect, but the actual truth. For Athens alone of all present-day cities exceeds her reputation in any enterprise she undertakes; she alone causes a belligerent enemy no irritation when he reflects by whom he is defeated, and arouses no resentment in her subjects that she is not fit to rule them. Our power is proved by many sure signs and an abundance of witnesses; it is an object of wonder to the present day and will be in the future.'

A Greek warrior taking leave of his parents.

A relief from the Acropolis at Athens of a trireme (a three-banked warship).

power gave them, and carried out long-distance naval operations. The result was a long deadlock, though the Athenians suffered terribly from plague at one time. A peace was made in 421 for a few years. But then the Athenians started the war again. A great expedition was planned against Syracuse, richest of the supporters of the Peloponnesian League. Not only was it a disaster – the Athenians lost half their army and all their fleet – but it decided the Spartans to ask the Persians for help. In return for a promise to restore the old Persian domination over the Greek cities of Asia, Persian money was supplied for a fleet to help the cities which wanted to shake off Athenian control. This time, after years of fighting, the destruction of the Athenian fleet, blockade and starvation, Athens was forced to give in.

Several things give this great struggle its importance. In the first place, it was unique in scale in Greek history. As Thucydides pointed out, turning back the earlier Persian invasions had been a matter of two sea battles and two on land. As for wars between Greek states, they were usually affairs of a short summer campaign ending in a battle between two hoplite

A cross-section of a trireme. Each trireme needed 170 rowers. There were usually thirty deck hands and only about fifteen soldiers, who directed ramming operations to try and sink enemy ships.

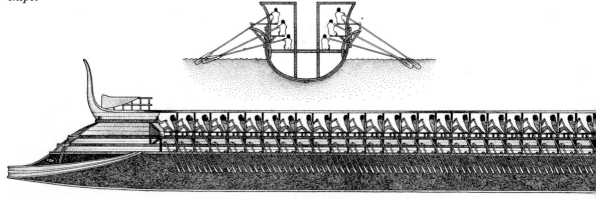

armies. This war was different. To cite Thucydides again, it was prolonged to an immense length, but, long as it was, it was unparalleled for the misfortunes it brought in a short time on the Hellenes.

The only gainers were the Persians. The Spartan victors were soon trying to bully other Greek states through their military might, as the Athenians had once dominated them through naval power. They had to fight coalitions in their turn. When the famed Spartan army was defeated at Leuctra in 371 BC, it was clear that Sparta was no more able than had been Athens to dominate the Greek cities and impose some sort of imperial unity upon them.

What the war showed, in fact, was that even the strongest of the Greek states was no longer able to enjoy unquestioned supremacy. The Greeks could neither keep out of one another's affairs nor accept the domination of any one *polis* over the rest. Perhaps Greek unity was bound to be impossible unless imposed by conquest, but no *polis* had enough power to carry that out. At the same time the Greek cities had in many cases long since ceased to be self-sufficient. They had many trading interests and had to be involved in politics over the whole length of the Greek world in order to look after them. Athens could not live without importing corn and exporting wine, oil and manufactures.

The war also threw great strains on the internal working of the *polis*. We have to be careful, because we know so much more about the history of some than of others, but at Athens, for example, the specialization required for prolonged warfare by both soldiers and sailors which led to the increasing use of mercenaries, the social divisions which appeared as a result of trade and were then made to seem unfair because of the way the war went, the bitterness which resulted from attacks on the politicians who had brought on disaster were all things which helped to produce a revolution which for a while replaced democracy with oligarchy. But something was going on which went deeper than just the replacement of one political regime by another. The old idea of the *polis* as essentially a unity of citizens all of whom took an equal part in all of its activities was no longer appropriate to the scale which the life of the state had come to have.

A Greek merchant ship from the sixth century BC, *very different from the later war galleys.*

Alexander the Great and his legacy

As the Greek states became feebler and less able to resist outside interferences, a new force began to make itself felt on the northern fringe of Hellas. This was the kingdom of Macedon.

Some people – Macedonian, for the most part – thought that Macedon was a Greek state and part of the Greek world. The Macedonians spoke Greek, after all, and attended Hellenic festivals. Their kings claimed to be descended from Greek families – from Achilles, the great Achaean hero of the *Iliad*, no less. But many Greeks thought the Macedonians were a barbarous lot, barely civilized, and certainly not on a par with the cultivated peoples of the city-states of the Aegean and Sicily. Undoubtedly Macedon was a rougher, tougher place than, say, Athens or Corinth and its kings had to dominate an aristocracy of mountain chiefs who would not have been much impressed by Socrates.

Macedon came to change the course of Greek history because of the coincidence of a number of favourable facts in the first half of the fourth century BC. One was an able and ambitious prince – ambitious, among other things, that Macedon should be recognized as a Greek state – who became regent in 359 BC. This was Philip II. At that moment circumstances were much in his favour; the Greek states were worn out by their long struggles and Persia had undergone a series of revolts which left her weak. Macedon was rich in gold and so could pay for a strong and effective army. But it was also an army which owed much to Philip's personal efforts. He had studied Greek military methods while at Thebes in his youth and had decided that the answer to hoplite tactics lay in a new formation, the phalanx. This was armed with pikes twice as long as ordinary spears and they were carried by ten ranks of soldiers who stood farther apart than hoplites so that the pikes of men in the rear stuck forward between the soldiers in the front two ranks. The result was a hedgehog-like array of points. Armoured cavalry and a siege-train of heavy weapons such as catapults backed up the phalanx and made the Macedonian army very formidable.

It was so good, indeed, that under Philip and his son it ended the independence of the mainland Greek cities. With that came the end of an era of human history, the age of the *polis*.

Alexander the Great's features appeared on coins minted in different parts of his empire. These three coins are from Crete, Alexandria and Pergamum (a city in present-day Turkey).

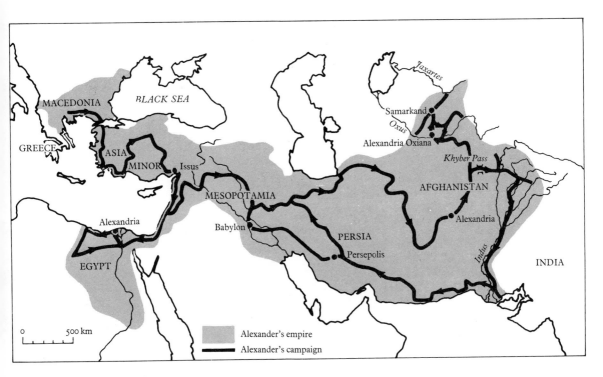

If a date marks it, 335 BC, when Thebes was razed to the ground and its inhabitants enslaved as a penalty for rebellion, will do. There were a few later revolts, but the great age of Greece was over. This might be enough in itself to ensure Macedon's kings a place in history, but there were more spectacular changes still to come. These were the work of Philip's son, Alexander.

Alexander is one of the few men in history who has traditionally been called 'Great'. So glamorous did he seem to his successors that legends galore surrounded his name and he was idolized for thousands of years. He was first and foremost a soldier and conqueror, but he was also much more. Unfortunately no contemporary biography of him survives and many of the facts of his life and personality remain obscure. Still, it is clear that he was a decisive force not only in Greek but in world history for about ten years, from 334 BC, when he crossed Asia to attack the Persians at the

head of an army drawn from many Greek states, to 323 BC, when he died in Babylon (perhaps of typhoid) only thirty-three years old.

Alexander was a passionate Hellene. He revered the memory of Achilles, his ancestor, had Aristotle as a tutor, and carried with him on his campaigns a treasured copy of Homer. He was a brave – and sometimes reckless – soldier as well as a shrewd general and a great leader of men who, once he had made conquests, could behave with sympathy to peoples whose rulers he overthrew. He was also violent; it seems he once killed a friend in a brawl while he was drunk. He may also have agreed to his father's murder.

Whatever his defects, they did not stop him achieving staggering success. He defeated the Persians in Asia Minor (the battle of Issus) and then marched through the length of their empire, first southwards through Syria to Egypt, then back north and east to Mesopotamia,

The Khyber Pass. Alexander instructed half of his army to enter India by way of this pass, while he with the rest of the troops were to cover its left flank from the hill country of Bajan and Swat.

pursuing the Persian king Darius III, who died while still on the run; this was the end of the Achaemenid empire. On went Alexander across Iran and Afghanistan, crossing the Oxus and going beyond Samarkand to found a city on the Jaxartes. Then he came south again, to invade India. Two hundred kilometres or so beyond the Indus, well into the Punjab, his weary generals made him turn back. A terrible march down the Indus and along the northern coast of the Persian Gulf followed until he reached Babylon. And there Alexander died.

He had done much more in his short life than merely fight. His 'empire' was soon to fall apart in the sense that it ceased to have a single centre of government, but he spread Greek influence where it had never been felt before. Alexander founded many cities (often named after him: there were several Alexandrias) and he mixed Greeks and Asians in his army so that they learnt from one another and became more cosmopolitan than before. Once he presided at a mass wedding of 9000 of his soldiers to eastern women, and he enlisted young Persian nobles in his cavalry. The former officials of the Persian king were kept in post to administer his conquered lands. Alexander even adopted Persian dress, and his Greek com-

The Macedonian phalanx was a formidable unit designed to break through the enemy's ranks, or take up defensive formation when under attack itself. Pikes held by the front ranks formed the attack, while soldiers behind held theirs up to deflect missiles.

panions did not like it when he took up the practice of making visitors to his court kowtow to him as they had done to the Persian king.

The most obvious things he had done, though, were to close the age of the autonomous Greek cities and overthrow the mightiest empire of his age, the Persian. These were very important deeds, though their full impact was not at once obvious. He did not have time to affect the history of the Greeks in the West, while the positive results of what he had done in Asia were only to appear after his death, when the effects would be felt in non-Greek lands of the Greek ideas and standards he

spread far and wide. This is why the word 'Hellenistic' is often applied both to the age which followed his death and to the area formerly covered by his empire (which was, roughly speaking, the zone between the Adriatic and Egypt in the west and the mountains of Afghanistan in the east). It did not hold together for long. Alexander left no heir who could take over from him and when he died his generals soon began fighting over the spoils. It took forty years or so for the lands of the former empire to settle down into a new pattern as a group of large states, each ruled by a king who was (or was descended from) one of

Right : the stories of Alexander's conquests gave rise to many legends and anecdotes. This illustration, of a priestess begging Alexander to stop the destruction of an idol, comes from a Persian manuscript of the sixteenth century.

A huge statue of Alexander from Egypt, depicting him as pharaoh.

Alexander's men. They are sometimes referred to as the 'Successors'.

The richest of these kingdoms was Egypt, where a Macedonian general named Ptolemy had seized control. He was able to get Alexander's body taken there and had it buried in a splendid tomb at Alexandria; this gave him special prestige and pre-eminence as its guardian. Ptolemy thus founded the last dynasty of the Egyptian kings of antiquity. The Ptolemies were to rule Egypt until 30 BC, when the last of the line, the famous Cleopatra, died.

Though the first Ptolemy's kingdom included Palestine, Cyprus and much of Libya, Egypt was not the biggest of the Successor states. The family of Seleucus, another Macedonian general, ruled one which stretched from Afghanistan (Alexander's Indian conquests had passed to an Indian king) to the Mediterranean. The Seleucid kingdom did not remain so large as this, though. Early in the third century BC a new kingdom of Pergamon was set up in Asia Minor, and in Bactria yet another kingdom was founded by Greek soldiers. Macedon itself, after being invaded by barbarians, had by then passed to a new dynasty, while the old Greek states, loosely organized from time to time in leagues, underwent a steady decline in the independence some of them had hoped to recover at Alexander's death.

The ups and downs of these Successor states do not matter much here. The difference they made to history was that they provided what Alexander's conquests had made likely – a framework within which Greek ideas and civilization took root as never before. Thanks to them, Greek became the official language of the whole Near East and more widely used as an everyday language too. It was spoken in particular in the new cities which were founded in great numbers (especially in the Seleucid territories) and to which Greek immigrants were encouraged to come.

These cities were very different from the cities of the Aegean. For one thing, they were much bigger. Alexandria in Egypt, Antioch in Syria and the Seleucid capital near Babylon each soon had nearly 200,000 inhabitants. Nor were they in any sense autonomous. The Seleucids, for example, governed through the machinery of provincial rulers, which they took over from the old Persian empire – a barbarian despotism in the eyes of fifth-century Greeks. Big civil services began to appear, and they drew on the age-old traditions of Egypt and Mesopotamia, not those of the *polis*. The rulers themselves were given semi-divine honours, like the old Persian kings. Indeed in Egypt the Ptolemies revived the old cult of the pharaohs, and the first Ptolemy took the title of 'Soter', that is 'Saviour'.

Still, the cities usually looked very Greek on the outside. Their buildings were in the Greek style. They had theatres, buildings for gymnastics, centres for games and festivals which were much like those of the past. Greek fashions spread and so did Greek culture. Soon Greek literature was being added to by writers in the new cities.

Life in the Hellenistic age was for a long time prosperous, partly because Alexander's wars had released an enormous booty in bullion and precious things which stimulated economic development in the towns. This pro-

vided taxation to pay for standing armies and bureaucracies. Altogether the Hellénistic world was a larger-scale affair than the old world of Hellas, and a broader stage for Greek culture, even though the countryside remained almost untouched by it. Most people in the Successor states did *not* speak Greek.

Greek tradition also continued in artistic style. Perhaps the best known of all Greek statues is the Aphrodite ('Venus de Milo') found on the island of Melos and now in the Louvre, Paris; this is a Hellenistic work. In science and learning too there was continuity with what had gone before. Egyptian Alexandria was pre-eminent in science. Euclid, the man who systematized geometry and gave it a shape which lasted to the nineteenth century, lived there. Among other Alexandrians were the first man to measure the size of the earth and the first to use steam to transmit energy. Archimedes, who is famous for constructing war-machines in Sicily, as well as for his theoretical discoveries in physics, was probably Euclid's pupil, and another Hellenistic Greek, Aristarchus (from Samos, this time, not Alexandria), even arrived at the view that the earth moved round the sun, and not vice versa (this idea was not accepted by his contemporaries, though, because it did not square with Aristotelian physics).

A body of knowledge and hypothesis such as this must be reckoned a big addition to the human toolkit. True, Hellenistic science was held back because there was neither the inclination nor the apparatus to test some of these theories experimentally and because there was a bias towards the mathematical sciences rather than the practical. It is also true that the existing state of technology made it impossible to make practical use of some ideas: effective steam-engines just could not be made until there were better and more accurate ways of boring cylinders, something that would not be mastered for many centuries.

The triumphs of Hellenistic science somewhat offset the loss of the tradition of self-government in politics and of the confident use of philosophy to seek answers to questions about the aims of life and the way men should behave. The Hellenistic world produced one important new ethical philosophy, Stoicism, which said, roughly, that it was men's duty to be virtuous whatever the consequences for themselves and that being virtuous consisted above all in obeying the natural laws which ruled the universe and all men, not just Greeks. This was the first attempt to provide a philosophy for all humanity. And it was to produce the first condemnation of slavery, an extraordinary step forward.

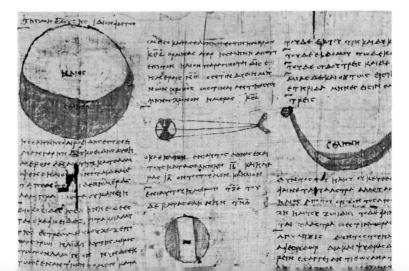

Opposite : the most famous of the many Alexandrias named after Alexander the Great is in Egypt. It was here that the famous lighthouse, considered one of the Seven Wonders of the World, was built. The lighthouse has completely disappeared, but we still have pictures of it on old medallions and coins.

Right : an Egyptian astronomical papyrus written in Greek in about the second century BC. *It is full of relatively simple explanatory diagrams.*

The rise of Roman power

After the expulsion of the Etruscan kings, around 510 BC, Rome was a republic, and her citizens were to go on insisting that this was so even when she looked much more like what we should call a monarchy. Realistically speaking, the Republic lasted about 450 years, until the middle of the first century BC. It changed a lot in this time, but one change was more important than others, because it explains Rome's impact on later history. This was the spread of Roman power. Even under the Republic, Roman rule was extended farther and farther until it came to encompass the whole Mediterranean world. This was the making of a Roman

Bronze figure of an African slave cleaning a boot.

Statue of a Roman consul in his toga.

A bronze statue of a Roman soldier wearing a cuirass to protect the upper part of his body.

empire which provided framework and cradle for developments that still shape our lives today.

While this was happening, much changed at home. During the first two centuries or so of the Republic violent political struggles took place, often because of the demands of the poorer citizens for a share in the power of the better-off and noble families. These 'patricians' dominated the Senate, which was the main governmental body, as the inscription carried on many monuments and on the standards of the army indicates: SPQR, the initials of the Latin words for 'the Roman Senate and People'. Yet somehow these struggles were carried on for a long time without mortal damage to the Republic. This says much for its institutions, which were slowly changed as concessions were made to popular forces. Yet, though the poorer citizens won many victories, Rome never became a democracy in the sense that they ever controlled the government for long.

For a long time the typical Roman citizen was a man of some independence. He was usually a peasant farming his own small property, benefiting from the splendid climate and fertility which have always made Italy potentially a rich country and showing the industry and skill with which later Italians have often demonstrated it to be so. His farming was the basis of the early Republic; we must not think of the huge metropolis of later centuries – living on imported corn and swollen by huge immigrant numbers – as typical of early Rome. Some new methods and new crops (the vine, for example) were introduced as the centuries went by, but for a long time the smallholder remained the typical Roman. Not until the second century BC did big estates owned by townsmen and relying on slave labour to grow cash crops of grain or olives (for

These later mosaics show Roman peasants sowing the fields and pruning vines. The labourers' costume was of necessity much more practical than the toga of the city dweller.

oil) become at all common in Italy. For a long time Romans would look back sentimentally to the simple days of the early Republic as the times when the Roman virtues were upheld by the independent smallholding citizens.

A narrow agricultural base therefore supported the first stage of Roman expansion. This makes it harder to explain. It would not be fair to say that Romans were always aggressive and anxious to make conquests. Often (as in later empires) Roman rule spread because of fear of neighbours and rivals rather than greed. Building an empire was a slow business, too. To start with, in the fifth century Rome's territory was doubled at the expense of her neighbours; in the immediate neighbourhood a Roman supremacy replaced the old Etruscan one. But this was not the beginning of a long uninterrupted success story; in 390 BC Gauls from the north sacked Rome itself (this was the famous occasion on which, according to legend, the Capitol to which the Romans had withdrawn was only saved from a surprise attack by the honking of the geese who noticed what was going on). Still, by about 250 BC the Romans came to dominate Italy south of the Arno; all of it by then belonged either to the Republic or to its allies. These allies were allowed to run their own internal affairs, but had to supply troops to the Roman army. In return their citizens enjoyed the rights of Roman citizens when they came to Rome. It was a little like the supremacy of Athens over her allies in the Delian League.

Roman success was built on several factors. Among them was the strategic position of the city. Then there was the distraction of the Etruscans, who were for a long time taken up in struggles with the Greeks and other Latin cities, while the Celtic tribes were pressing them in the north. Another factor was a military system which made the best of Rome's manpower. Every male citizen who owned property had to serve in the army if needed. This was no light demand; an infantryman had to serve sixteen years under the early Republic, though service was not for the whole year, since campaigns started in spring and finished during the autumn. Yet it provided a military machine which became the finest the world had seen in the next few centuries. The pool of recruits on which the army drew grew steadily because of the obligations of allies to send contingents to it.

In the process of taking over all Italy, Rome had become involved with powers farther afield. Some of the Greek cities had called in the king of Epirus to help them against the Romans. He had campaigned in the south and Sicily, thinking perhaps of building himself an empire in the west like Alexander's. He won battles all right, but at such a cost that we still talk of 'Pyrrhic victories' (his name was Pyrrhus) as ones which cost more than they are worth. At one time, too, it looked as if Ptolemaic Egypt might want Rome's alliance.

The first great preoccupation of the Republic outside Italy in fact did lie in Africa, though farther west than Egypt. The Phoenician city of Carthage was a great naval power, with outposts in Sicily and Sardinia. It was at times allied to and at times at war with the Greeks of Sicily, and was always a standing menace to the rich western coastal plains of Italy and to any possibility of building up trade in their ports.

In the end three 'Punic' (the name comes from the Latin word for Phoenician) wars were fought by Rome and Carthage. The first ended in 241 BC with the Carthaginians having to give up Sicily; Syracuse was forced to abandon its alliance with them. More than twenty years of fighting were needed for this, though of course it was not continuous. The Romans also took control of Corsica and Sardinia as a result, and they founded their first Roman province in western Sicily (mainland Italy was either governed directly as part of the Republic or was technically allied to it). These were the first acquisitions of overseas territory by Rome.

Wars are by no means always the most

important events at any particular time, but in this instance it is worthwhile to stick to the story of the Punic wars for a little longer because so much followed from them. The second began in 218 BC and went very badly for the Romans at first. The Carthaginians had established themselves in Spain, starting at 'New Carthage' (the modern Cartagena) and had begun to alarm the Romans when their power extended as far as the Ebro. The actual cause of the war was a Carthaginian attack on one of the few remaining independent cities on the Spanish coast, and this was followed by the march of a Carthaginian army – complete with elephants – to Italy under Hannibal, the greatest Carthaginian general. A series of bad defeats for the Romans followed. Many of their allies changed sides. But the Romans hung on. In the end they recovered their grip. The Carthaginians were starved and driven out after twelve years in Italy. The Roman Senate gave their successful general, Scipio,

This Etruscan plate from the third century BC, *the age of Hannibal, shows the elephant being used as a beast of war.*

A silver coin, minted in Spain, showing Hannibal.

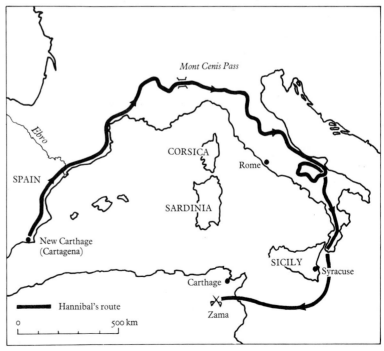

permission to cross to Africa, and at Zama in 202 BC he finally defeated the Carthaginians. This was one of the decisive battles of history – one which made a difference to the fate of the world – because it broke the back of Rome's only serious rival in the West.

The Carthaginians had to make a crippling peace. But many Romans still feared them mightily. A third Punic war did not break out for a long time – until 149 BC – but it ended with so complete a defeat for the Carthaginians that their city was destroyed and ploughs were run over the site where it had stood. But by that time everything had changed in the western Mediterranean and had begun to change in the east too. By then the Roman empire was in being, in fact if not in name.

The overthrow of Carthage had meant the end of Syracuse, the last independent Greek state in Sicily, because she had once more allied with the Carthaginians. All Sicily was now Roman. Southern Spain too was conquered. Soon slaves and gold from Sicily, Sardinia and Spain were making some Romans aware that conquests might be profitable. The Punic wars had effects in the East too. Macedon had allied with Carthage for a time, and so Rome had begun to dabble in Greek politics by making friends with Greek cities opposed to Macedon. In 200 BC a direct appeal for help against Macedon and the Seleucids was made by Athens and the kingdom of Pergamon, and the Romans were by then ready psychologically to become further involved in the East.

The second century BC was crucial. Macedon was overthrown, the Greek cities were reduced to vassalage, the last king of Pergamon bequeathed his land to Rome in 133 BC. A new province, Asia (the western end of Anatolia) was set up in the same year. By then northern Spain had been conquered too. Soon after, southern France was taken. In the next century northern France followed and then further conquests in the East. This was an astonishing success story and it was not only Rome which drew benefits from it. But there was a high cost to be paid for these successes.

The eagle became an emblem of the might of Rome when Marius capped the standards of the Roman Legions with silver eagles in 104 BC.

As its great harbour suggests, Carthage was a formidable naval power, and to fight her Rome had to build a fleet which could carry legionaries. This relief shows a Roman ship in the first century BC with soldiers preparing for hand-to-hand fighting.

How Carthage might have looked in the second century BC. The drawing based on written descriptions that has come down to us shows the city's greatest feature — the round naval harbour with its colonnade of Greek Ionic columns.

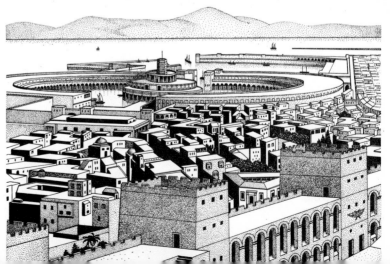

The decay of the Republic

The Romans liked to congratulate themselves for following what they called *mos maiorum* – 'the ways of our ancestors' would be a reasonable translation of this Latin phrase. They always showed a fondness for old traditions and liked to keep alive old ways of doing things. Even Roman religion was in large measure a matter of making sure that ancient ceremonies were kept up and carried out in the proper manner. When they did something new, the Romans liked to wrap it up in older packaging. The result was that the names of many of the Republic's institutions – and the idea that the state was a republic and not a monarchy – went on being used long after they ceased to mean much in practice.

Roman citizenship is an example. The first citizens were usually peasant freeholders with the right to vote and get justice before the courts, and the duty of serving in the army. Three important changes came about as the centuries went by. In the first place, rights of citizenship were gradually given to many people outside the original Roman territories. Secondly, the Punic wars impoverished the Italian peasant. Conscription took Roman soldiers away from their homesteads and families, which often fell into poverty as a result, and the wars also did enormous damage in the countryside of southern Italy. When peace at last returned, many former smallholders could not make a living there. On the other hand, men who had been lucky enough to make money out of the wars began to buy up land for farming in big estates. Slaves (part of the booty of conquest) often were used to

A banquet scene from a Roman sepulchral monument.

A draper's shop. The customers of rank remain seated with their servants standing beside them, while the traders display a piece of cloth to them.

work these and so the citizen-peasant tended to drift to the city to find a living there as best he could. He was on the way to being what the Romans called a 'proletarian' – someone whose only contribution to the state was to breed children.

Both these changes affected politics. More poor citizens meant more voters to be bought, cajoled or bullied by politicians anxious to get into positions which would give them a chance to get at the rich prizes offered by conquest abroad.

The third thing which altered the meaning of citizenship also stemmed from war: the army became more and more a full-time professional force, rather than one of citizens temporarily in uniform. One landmark was the ending of a property qualification for service; as more and more citizens were propertyless, the pool of Roman military manpower had been showing signs of drying up. If the propertyless could serve, sufficient volunteers

would come forward from among the poor who were willing to serve for pay, so that conscription now became hardly necessary. True, for some time the recruit still had to be a citizen, but in the end non-citizens were allowed to join up. They then received rights of citizenship as a reward for their service.

Gradually, in these ways, the Roman army grew apart from the Republic. The famed legions in which it was organized became permanent organizations, whose soldiers increasingly felt loyalty to their comrades and their generals. From the first century BC each legion carried 'eagles' – standards which symbolized the honour and unity of the legion, a sort of combination of a religious idol and a regimental badge.

A mass of impoverished citizens with votes to be bought; opportunities for politicians to get at wealth on a huge scale in the new territories to which they could be appointed as governors and generals; an army which was

Right: a country scene from a sarcophagus. The goatherd is milking his goat under what seems to be a screen put up to protect him from the weather.

A realistic interior of a butcher's shop. The chopping block and cuts of meat are similar to those seen in butchers' shops today. The person on the left is probably the book-keeper.

unbeatable (or almost) in the field and more and more loyal to itself and its leaders rather than to the Senate – these were the slow but crucial political changes, and they went on for nearly two centuries. They transformed the Republic under the surface even though much still looked the same.

Meanwhile great changes were taking place in other ways too. For one thing, Rome was obviously getting richer. This was not just a matter of the loot and slaves conquests offered to a few lucky enough to be in the right place at the right time. Poor citizens also benefited indirectly; new provinces were taxed and so taxation ceased at home. Some wealth also went into the beautifying of Rome and other Italian cities.

Other changes followed more contact with the East, especially with the Greek cities whose cultural past was, after all, what educated Romans were brought up to respect as the roots of their own. It brought fashions and standards to the West which reinforced the influence of the old western Greek cities. So the process of Hellenization spread farther. It showed in everyday things as well as in art and intellectual life; the Romans' passion for bathing now seems one of the most remarkable things about them, but in fact they took the fashion from the Hellenistic East.

The spread of Roman rule under the Republic provides a contrast to the growing corruption and violence in politics at home. Bad though some Roman provincial governors might have been, it was a fact that Roman power brought peace to a larger area of the

It was under the emperor Trajan that the Roman Empire reached its greatest extent before its decline. Trajan's column, a memorial to his victories in Dacia (roughly in present-day

Mediterranean and Near East and did so for longer periods than ever before. Republican administration imposed order over many peoples and provided a common law for running their affairs. Many of those who lived under Roman rule and were not Roman nevertheless admired it. They praised some of those who ran the system, admiring them for their sense of justice, disinterestedness and the civilizing work they did. The outcome was very important for the history of the world too. Already, when the Republic came to an end, there existed a political and military framework on a scale without parallel west of Han China. It protected Hellenistic civilization. Many different cultures could live side by side within it and make their own contributions to the cosmopolitan whole.

An illustration on a vase showing a Gaul hunting with bow and arrows.

Romania), shows many scenes from the campaign. Here we have soldiers building a fort and others, bearing their standards, crossing a bridge.

This structure went on growing. In 58 BC the Romans annexed Cyprus. In the next few years a young politician called Julius Caesar took command of the Roman army in Gaul (France) and finished off the independence of the Celtic peoples there. (He also led two reconnaissance expeditions across the Channel to the island Romans called Britannia, but did not stay.) These can be regarded as the last additions to the Republic's territories. By 50 BC all the northern coasts of the Mediterranean, all France and the Low Countries, all Spain and Portugal, a substantial chunk of the southern Black Sea coast and much of modern Tunisia and Libya were under Roman rule. Yet the Republic was then on the verge of disappearance.

The roots of collapse have already been described, but the way it happened owed much to individuals. Round about 100 BC emergencies in Africa and southern Gaul led to generals – who were politicians wearing different hats – being given exceptional powers. They used these against their political opponents as well as the Republic's enemies. In Italy restiveness among Rome's allies led first to war on them and then to the extension of Roman citizenship to virtually the whole of Italy – which made nonsense of the idea that the Roman popular assemblies (which only met at Rome) had the last word in the Republic.

Julius Caesar landed in Britain on 25 August 55 BC. He stayed three weeks and came back again the following year for a two-month campaign. He brought the island within the Roman sphere of influence; after him there is plenty of evidence of contact until finally the emperor Claudius chose to invade Britain in AD 43. Julius Caesar's motives were probably personal – he was an ambitious soldier and politician out for glory. To ensure his deeds were not overlooked, he wrote his own accounts of them, including this description of his first landing, probably near what is now Deal, in Kent:

These matters settled, he waited for a suitable wind and set sail about midnight. The cavalry were ordered to go to another harbour to embark and follow him. This they were rather slow to do, and so it was about 10 am when he arrived off Britain with the leading ships. Armed men could be seen stationed on all the heights, and the nature of the place was such, with the shore edged by sheer cliffs, that missiles could be hurled onto the beach from the top. Caesar considered this a totally unsuitable place for disembarkation, and waited at anchor till 3 pm for the rest of his invasion fleet to assemble. He then summoned a meeting of his brigade and battalion commanders, revealed the news he had from Volusenus, and outlined his orders. He wanted them to be ready to act immediately, on the slightest sign from him. For military practice demanded this, especially in a naval attack, which was liable to rapid, unexpected changes of circumstance. Dismissing his officers, he waited for a favourable combination of wind and tide, and then gave the signal to weigh anchor. Sailing on for about seven miles, he halted his line opposite an open, level beach.

The barbarians had discovered Caesar's plan by sending forward cavalry units and charioteers (a very common method of fighting with them). Their main force which had followed later was now in a position to prevent our men from disembarking. This caused considerable difficulty. The ships could only be drawn up in deep water because of their draught. The soldiers were faced with unknown ground and had their hands impeded, while they were burdened with a very heavy load of arms. And yet they had to leap down from the ships, keep their footing in the waves and fight the enemy. The latter, on the other hand,

could resist either from dry land or by moving just a little forward into the shallows. So, completely unencumbered and with full knowledge of the ground, they boldly hurled their missiles, badly disturbing the horses which were totally unused to the conditions. Our men were shaken by these circumstances through lack of experience of this style of warfare, and failed to show the same dash and enthusiasm as they did in land battles.

As Caesar noticed this, he gave orders to the warships to row off slightly to the enemy's open flank away from the cargo ships. These ships were less well known to the barbarians and much more manoeuvrable. They were to halt, attack and move the enemy back by the use of slings, arrows and other missiles. All this helped our men considerably. The barbarians were affected by the strange shape of the ships, by the motion of the oars and the unusual type of catapult. Halting their advance, they slowly began to retire.

Our troops, however, were still hesitating, largely because of the depth of the sea, when the standard-bearer of the Tenth legion, with a prayer to the gods for a happy outcome for his legion, shouted, 'Jump down, men, unless you want the enemy to get your standard. You will not find me failing in my duty to my country or my leader.' This he yelled at the top of his voice, and then springing off the boat began to bear the eagle forward against the enemy. Our troops, with mutual words of encouragement not to commit a terrible wrong, all jumped down into the sea. Their fellows in the next boats saw what they were doing, followed suit and came to grips with the enemy.

A Roman coin showing Julius Caesar.

More wars in the East threw up yet more war-lords who turned out to have political ambitions at home. Rome became a dangerous place – to political intrigue and corruption were now added murder and mob violence. People began to fear the emergence of a dictator, but were not sure where he was to come from.

Somewhat unexpectedly it turned out to be Julius Caesar. His seven years in Gaul gave him three great advantages; he was away from Rome while other people were blamed for the increasing disorder, violence and corruption there; he became enormously rich; and he won the loyalty of the best-trained and most experienced of the Roman armies. His soldiers felt that he was a man who would look after them, assuring them pay, promotion and victory.

Caesar has always been a fascinating figure. He has been seen both as a hero and as a villain, and his reputation has swung about. He did not have a very long career at the top, and it finished at the hands of his enemies, yet few have questioned his abilities. True, he helped

to give people a good idea of them by writing his own accounts of his successful campaigns in some of the best Latin of his day. Whatever his aims and however we judge the morality of what he did, it can at least be agreed that, in the first place, he was no worse than most other politicians of his day and often showed himself better, and secondly that he had great qualities of leadership, cool-headedness and determined patience. Though not cruel, he was ruthless. Once he was captured by some pirates who held him to ransom. He used to joke and play dice with them while he waited for his release and while he did so he teased them by saying he would crucify them one day. The pirates laughed. Caesar was freed and, sure enough, crucify them in due course he did.

In January 49 BC Caesar struck at last. Claiming to be defending the Republic from its enemies, he crossed the River Rubicon, the border of his province, and began to march with his army to Rome – an illegal act. For four years he campaigned in Africa, Spain and Egypt, chasing his opponents who had armies in the provinces which they might use against

This scene from Trajan's Column shows the testudo *(or tortoise) formation in which Roman soldiers held their shields over their heads for protection during a charge or ramming operation.*

him. He crushed opposition by force but also won over former enemies by mildness after success. He carefully organized his political support in the Senate and was made dictator for life. But some Romans feared that Caesar might re-establish a monarchy. In the end his enemies came together and in 44 BC he was murdered in the Senate.

What had changed by then? In form, not much. The Republic was still there. But in fact the changes Caesar had already made in the direction of centralized power were left intact and no one tried to solve political problems by putting the clock back. In the end it was Caesar's great-nephew and adopted heir, Octavian, who made it clear that there had been an irreversible change. Thus began what we know as the Roman empire.

Octavian spent some time hunting down the politicians who had murdered Caesar. He then fought a civil war which took him as far afield as Egypt (it was duly annexed as a province, the line of the Ptolemies coming to an end with the legendary suicides of Anthony and Cleopatra). When he returned to Rome supported by the loyalty of his old soldiers (and those of his great-uncle), he used his power carefully, getting the Senate to provide a cloak of republican respectability for everything he did. He was, formally speaking, only *imperator* – a title that meant he commanded soldiers in the field – but he was made consul year after year and was in due course given the honorary title of 'Augustus'; it is as Caesar Augustus that he has gone down in history. His power grew as more and more offices and honours were given

---

The Julio-Claudian emperors

27 BC–AD 14	Augustus (Octavian)
14–37	Tiberius
37–41	Gaius
41–54	Claudius
54–68	Nero

The Flavian and Antonine emperors

69	'Year of the Four Emperors' (Galba, Otho, Vitellius, Vespasian)
69–79	Vespasian
79–81	Titus
81–96	Domitian
96–8	Nerva
98–117	Trajan
117–38	Hadrian
138–61	Antoninus Pius
161–80	M. Aurelius and L. Verus
180–93	Commodus

Augustus *was Caesar's great-nephew and really the first Roman emperor; more likenesses of him survive than of any other Roman ruler. He was a master of propaganda, and spreading about images of himself on coins, jewels and monuments was one of his techniques. In form he upheld the Republic still, but in practice he never showed any intention of laying down his power.*

Tiberius *was a conscientious and careful ruler. But because he was economical (and, in particular, hardly spent any money on public games) he was not popular. In the end he seems not to have been able to stand up to the strains of his office. He went in fear of assassination and retired to Capri for safety for the last ten years of his reign, where he seems to have more or less gone mad.*

to him, but he never ceased to insist that this was all within the old republican framework. He was *princeps* – first citizen – not a king.

In reality, of course, the rules had changed. Instead of playing politics, Augustus increasingly relied on the real power given him by control of the army (he was the first man to organize a regiment for service in the capital itself, the Praetorian Guard) and on a bureaucracy of paid civil servants. He intended to be succeeded by a kinsman and though this was only an adopted stepson (his own child was a daughter) five Caesars in a row became *imperator* and *princeps* after him. And, after he died in AD 14, Augustus was declared a god – as had been Julius Caesar.

This was a big change. It settled the Roman state on a new course. It would be ruled in future by monarchs, though they would depend on, and therefore need to please, the army. The empire (as we may now call it) was to bring great achievements and would spread Roman rule even farther, but it too was to fail in the end.

What had changed by the time Augustus died was the centuries-old domination of Rome by a relatively small class of politicians. It had ended with the triumph of one of the leading families among them. Not that the family of the Caesars was to enjoy an untroubled ascendancy. Augustus went to his grave to be remembered as the great bringer of peace and restorer of old Roman ways. But none of the three Caesars who followed his successor, Tiberius, died a natural death – and some have thought that Tiberius did not either.

Nero – *vain, egoistic, cruel and revengeful, there is not much good to be said of him. He arranged for his mother (with whom he is shown here) and first wife to be murdered and he executed scores of imagined or real opponents. But he was almost certainly not responsible for the great fire of AD 64, which wiped out half the city of Rome and which he was said to have both started and gloated over while reciting his own poems.*

Hadrian, *like Trajan, who had adopted him as his successor, was born in Spain. He worked hard to stabilize the frontier (Hadrian's Wall is one of his best-known monuments). He was a cultivated man who wrote verses. Like some earlier emperors, he made great use of his image on coins to encourage the provinces to look to him as protector and thus strengthen central authority in the Empire.*

Marcus Aurelius, *as a boy, was a favourite of Hadrian. He was an intellectual, devoted to Stoic philosophy, who left a famous book of* Meditations *– a devotional work – and yet lived much of his reign campaigning as a soldier. He was much mourned when he died, but, more through bad luck than bad management, left the empire in worse shape than he found it.*

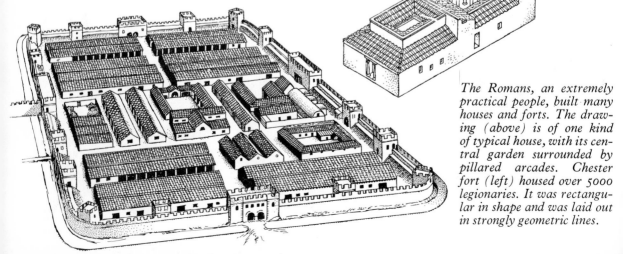

BRITANNIA

GAUL

Rhine

Marseilles

SPAIN

Ebro

Corsica

Sardinia

Carthage

Rome ITALY

Rubicon ILLYRICUM

Sicily

Syracuse

Danube

MACEDONIA

BLACK SEA

ASIA

Cyprus

SYRIA

CYRENE

Alexandria

AFRICA

EGYPT

0   500km

Roman empire 44 BC

How the empire grew in the century and a half between the deaths of Julius Caesar in 44 BC and Trajan AD 117.

The Romans, an extremely practical people, built many houses and forts. The drawing (above) is of one kind of typical house, with its central garden surrounded by pillared arcades. Chester fort (left) housed over 5000 legionaries. It was rectangular in shape and was laid out in strongly geometric lines.

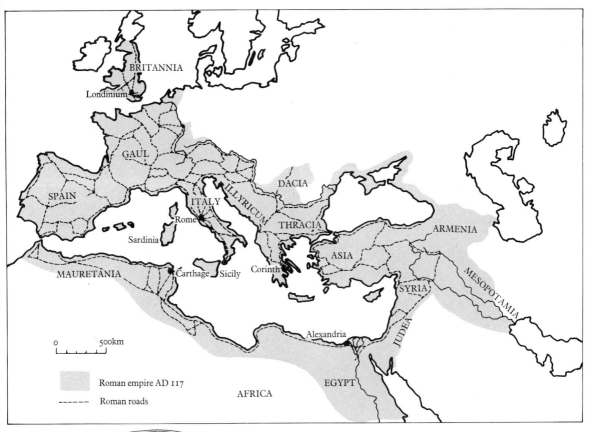

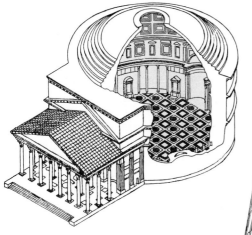

The Pantheon was a temple dedicated to the gods. It was built in about AD 125, with a stone dome over fifty metres across.

They also built many spectacular public buildings, particularly in Rome itself. The Colosseum (below) was begun under Vespasian and opened in AD 80. It held about 80,000 spectators, who came to watch gladiatorial fights and other sports – including Christians being mauled by lions. A huge canvas awning protected spectators from rain and sun.

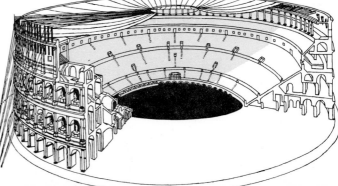

The coming of Christianity

Much time can be spent – by no means wastefully – in arguing about what we mean by 'important' in history. Still, one commonsense view is that something is historically important if it affects the lives of a great many people. On this reckoning, we can safely say that no single event in ancient times and probably none in the whole of human history is as important as the birth of Jesus. We can be fairly certain this was in Nazareth, in Palestine, and slightly less

sure when it happened, though 6 BC seems the most likely date. The whole of human history since shows how important it was. Quite simply, those who later called themselves Christians – the followers of Jesus – were to change the history of the whole globe. To find something which has had a comparable effect we have to look not to single events but to big processes like industrialization, or the great forces of prehistoric times like climate which set the stage for history.

This has not saved people from violent disagreement about Jesus and about what he was trying to do. But it can be seen easily enough that what gave the teaching of Jesus a much greater impact than that of other holy men of his age was that his followers saw him crucified and yet believed he later rose again from the dead. They were Palestinian Jews, and to understand the story of Jesus we have to set him in the history of the Jews, his people.

Since the Exile in 587 BC, to which the Babylonians carried off many Jews, and the destruction of the Temple at Jerusalem, much had happened to make the Jewish nation feel even more distinctive and even more unlike other Near Eastern peoples. Deprived of the Temple as a centre for their cult, the Jews had turned to weekly reading of their scriptures (which made up much of what we now call the Old Testament), a practice which led in time to the appearance of the synagogue, a place where teaching and reading, not sacrifice, went on. Furthermore the prophets who had led some of the Jews back from Exile in 538 BC (after the Persian overthrow of Babylon) had preached a more exact and narrow observation of the Jewish law, in order to set Jews apart from other peoples, the 'gentiles', and had made sure the Temple was rebuilt. When Palestine was under Seleucid rule some Jews had taken to Hellenistic ways, but they belonged to an upper-class minority often distrusted and disliked by the people, who clung unquestioningly to their tradition – and indeed became even more tenacious of it. There was a great Jewish revolt in the second century BC against 'Hellenization'. After this the Seleucid kings treated the Jews very cautiously.

A period of independence for about eighty years followed the end of Seleucid rule in 143 BC. Then Judaea was taken by Rome. Two thousand years were to pass before there was again an independent Jewish state in the Middle East. By the time of Augustus, though, fewer Jews lived in Judaea than in the rest of the Roman empire. After the Exile the freedom of movement and trade offered first by the Hellenistic states and then by the rule of Rome had spread Jews all round the Mediterranean coasts, into the Black Sea ports and into Mesopotamia. This was the 'Dispersion'. Some even settled in the ports of Western India by

about 175 BC. In some Roman cities there were huge numbers of them; at Rome itself there may have been 50,000 and there was another great Jewish centre in Alexandria.

Jewish numbers also grew slightly from the conversion of gentiles. They were drawn to Judaism by its moral code, by religious ceremonies which centred round reading the scriptures and did not need shrines or priests, and above all because it promised human salvation. The Jewish view of history was clear and inspiring; it saw the Jewish people as one set apart by God, a chosen people who would be refined in the fire for the Day of Judgement, but who would then be gathered to salvation. Yet relations between Jews and their neighbours were often strained. Rioting was not uncommon and troubled the Roman authori-

A mosaic showing Christ and his disciples at the Last Supper before his betrayal to the Roman authorities. This supper is now recalled in the Christian Mass or communion service.

ties. Popular prejudices were easily aroused by Jewish distinctiveness and success.

In AD 26 a new Roman governor, Pontius Pilate, was appointed to the province of which Judaea was a part. This was a bad moment in its history, when it was especially disturbed. The Jews of Syria and Palestine were divided against one another, hated their Greek and Syrian neighbours, and most of all hated the Roman occupiers and their tax-gatherers. Some Jews belonged to a sect called Zealots who were in a sense a resistance movement.

About thirty years earlier Jesus had been born. Many of his countrymen were at that moment waiting for a leader, a 'Messiah', one anointed by God, and a descendant of the line of David, who would take them forward to victory – whether military or symbolic there was much disagreement. Jesus grew up amid these expectations. He knew himself to be a holy man and his teaching and the miracles reported of him awoke great excitement. Of his life we have the Gospels as a record, the accounts written down after his death by fol-

This stone, recording the dedication of a building to the Roman emperor by Pontius Pilate, then governor of Palestine, provides the only direct evidence of Pilate's existence.

lowers, on the basis of the actual memory of those who had known him. The Gospels were written, of course, to show that they were right in thinking him a unique person – Messiah.

His uniqueness was demonstrated for them by what happened at the end of Jesus' life. He was charged with blasphemy by the Jewish religious leaders and taken before the Roman governor, Pilate. Anxious to avoid further communal strife in a troubled city, Pilate bent the letter of the law somewhat and allowed him to be condemned. So Jesus was crucified, probably in AD 33. Soon afterwards his disciples believed that he had risen from the dead, that they had met him and talked to him after that, that they had seen him ascend into heaven and that he had left them only to return soon sitting at the right hand of God to judge all men at the end of time.

Whatever may be thought of the details of the Gospel records, it cannot plausibly be maintained that they were written by men who did not believe these things nor that they did not write down what they were told by men who believed they had seen them with their own eyes. Clearly, too, Jesus' life was not so successful in a worldly sense that his teaching was likely to survive because of the impact of his ethical message alone. He had, it is true, especially attracted many of the poor and outcast, as well as Jews who felt that their traditions in the forms into which they had hardened were no longer wholly satisfactory. But these successes would have died with him had his disciples not believed that he had conquered death itself and that those who were saved by being baptized as his followers would also overcome death and live for ever after God's judgement.

Before a century had passed, this message was being preached throughout the whole civilized world sheltered by the Roman empire. It took root first in Jewish communities, and for this reason the earlier dispersion was of great importance in setting the pattern of early

Christianity (a word we take from the Greek name soon given to Jesus – the 'Christ', or 'anointed one'). Soon Jesus was also preached to the gentiles. This was the decision of a council of 'Christians' (the word was by then beginning to be used of followers of Jesus) held at Jerusalem in AD 49. Besides those who had known him personally (Jesus' brother James and his disciple, Peter, among them) there also may have been present a Hellenized Jew from Tarsus who is the most important figure after Jesus himself in the spread of Christianity: Saul, known later as St Paul. Many gentiles were already interested in the new teaching, but it was the combination of Paul's missionary work and the decision of the Jerusalem Council that gentiles should not be asked to conform to the Jewish law – that is, accept the full rigour of the Jewish religion, and show it by undergoing circumcision – which released the most successful of world religions from the Jewish shell which had protected its earliest life.

Paul was also important in another way. Christianity not only now began to emerge from Jewish society, but through him from the world of Jewish ideas. Much that was Jewish remained to future Christianity, of course. So far as we know, Jesus had at no time in his teaching gone beyond the intellectual world of the law and the prophets, and was scrupulous in his own religious observances. Paul, a Greek-speaker and an educated man, nevertheless put his view of Jesus' message into Greek and, in the process, into the language and ideas of Greek philosophy. Greek ideas of the distinction between soul and body, of the links between the visible, material world and the invisible, spiritual world were used by him to preach his message. He outraged orthodox Jews by preaching a Jesus who was God himself; such an idea could never find a place within Judaism.

It is not too much to say that most of the theology of the Christian Church has its roots

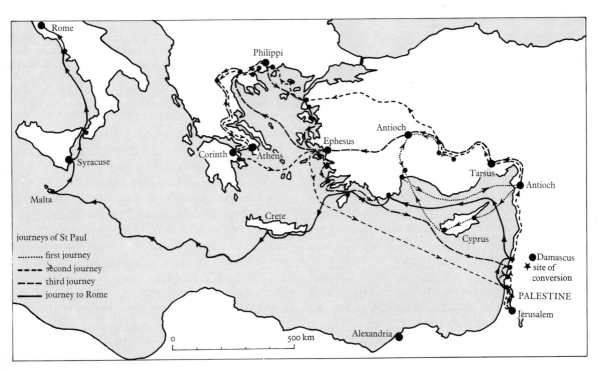

journeys of St Paul
.... first journey
- - - - second journey
– – – third journey
——— journey to Rome

Although the political situation in the empire meant that Christianity could spread quite easily, its devotees had to grapple with their neighbours' loyalties to many different gods worshipped at the time. This is a household shrine from Pompeii. Most households had their own gods who watched over the home and family.

Right: the Greek goddess Artemis (known to the Romans as Diana) was originally worshipped as a mother-goddess and fertility symbol. She was incorporated into later, more masculine-oriented religions when she became known as the huntress. This famous statue is of Diana of Ephesus, whose many breasts (or perhaps eggs) denote her status as a mother-goddess.

in Paul's teaching. Here there is room only to note that he seized the opportunity presented by a world at peace, protected by a framework of government and law in which men could travel easily and securely, a world in which the widespread Greek language made communication of ideas easy, to launch Christianity on its huge career of expansion. It is not surprising that Christians soon began to think that the Roman empire itself was somehow created by God to make the spreading of the Truth possible: it was meant, they thought, to further Christianity. A more sinister thought also occurred to some of them as time passed: it was not the Romans, after all, but the Jews

who had actually killed Jesus. On this distinction (as well as on many other sources) anti-semitism was later to thrive.

Almost the last thing we know of Paul is that when he was accused by the Jewish leaders at Jerusalem of sedition and profanation of the Jewish temple, he used his rights as a Roman citizen to appeal from the judgement of the governor at Caesarea to the emperor at Rome. To the capital he made his way to await trial. What happened to him after that we do not actually know. According to early Christian tradition, he was martyred at Rome in AD 67. Whatever the truth about this, he had by then changed history.

This altar, showing a sacrifice, was dedicated to the cult of the emperor and was found in the temple of Vespasian in Pompeii.

A painting from Herculaneum showing priests of Isis performing the ceremony of the water.

Other civilizations

Beyond the Roman frontiers lay mysterious but not entirely unknown lands. When Ptolemy, a second-century Alexandrian Greek, compiled an atlas which showed a remarkably accurate knowledge of the area covered by the empire, it was much vaguer about what lay beyond its frontiers. On his map, Africa straggled off beyond Libya into a vast 'Aethiopia'; India was there, with its two great river valleys, but much smaller than it should have been in relation to the island now called Srilanka. Farther away still lay the mysterious land which the Romans were to call 'Serica' – China.

With all these places the Roman world was in touch, though often only just and indirectly. Christianity may have reached the western Indian ports in the first century AD, and kings lived in Ceylon who had bodyguards of Roman soldiers (foreign mercenaries were always useful for such purposes, as the employment of Greek soldiers by the Persian kings, and Anglo-Saxons and Norsemen by later Byzantine emperors, showed). From China came silk – hence the name 'Serica', which means 'silken' in Latin – and from India pepper and spices. Perfume and gums were imported from Arabia, and ivory and timber from sub-Saharan Africa. Yet there was virtually no contact between the political authorities of these distant lands and the Roman emperors.

Given the communications of the day, that is hardly surprising. As a result, though, different parts of the world followed almost completely independent courses of development at least until the beginning of the modern age – say, the sixteenth century AD – when they began to be somewhat more pulled together. The two most important areas where different styles of civilization continued to evolve in this way were China and India.

China

For over four hundred years, from 206 BC to AD 220, China was ruled by emperors of two dynasties with the same name – the Han. For a short period (AD 9–23) the 'former' Han ceased to reign and the 'later' Han had not succeeded them, but the two eras can for our purposes be thought of as a whole. Having said that, though, we must be careful about what we mean by 'ruled'. This is not just because some individual emperors were much more vigorous and effective than others, though that was true. It is also because it is easy to exaggerate the extent of government at all times in early China. The boundary of the Han empire on the map is a pretty theoretical affair; control was certainly not achieved over the whole area within it in the sense that Rome ruled her empire.

Nor did Chinese civilization dominate what we now call China in the way Hellenistic civilization dominated western Europe, the Mediterranean and the Near East. Chinese script had only been standardized under the Ch'in (just before Han times). A tribal society in which only a few leading men were 'sinicized' (that is, had taken to Chinese ways) was the rule over much of the area politically subjected to the Han, especially in the south. There was still not much basic cement for the regime.

Nevertheless some of the Han emperors extended China's claims to political domination farther than any of their predecessors. In theory at least, the Han empire was, at its greatest extent, as big as the Roman. The emperor Wu Ti, the 'Martial Emperor' who reigned 141–87 BC, was especially acquisitive. Under him a big area of Central Asia, the Tarim Basin, was taken into the empire, as well as southern Manchuria – land north of the

Great Wall – and much of the south-eastern coast of China. The Thai peoples of the Mekong Valley were also subjugated and Annam accepted the overlordship of the Han. Later, Mongolian peoples called the Hsing-Nu (we shall meet them elsewhere later under the more familiar name of 'Huns') were driven north of the Gobi Desert.

Expansion increased China's contacts with other peoples, though those with the Mediterranean remained only indirect. Most of China's trade was by land and the most desirable commodity she produced was silk. From about 100 BC it was being sent to the west by caravans along the 'Silk Road' of Central Asia. Perhaps the new contacts of this era with the nomads of the deserts explain the appearance of the beautiful bronze horses which began to be cast in Han times.

Yet, in spite of wider boundaries, China remained remarkably untouched by influences from outside. Nothing like Judaism's effect through Christianity on Graeco-Roman civilization can be detected. Even Buddhism (which appears to have made its way to China during the first century AD along the trade-routes from Central Asia) was seen under the Han as an exotic import, a religion for foreigners.

Educated Chinese already thought of their country as the centre of the world and the seat of true civilization; this intellectual arrogance no doubt explains much of China's isolation from what was going on elsewhere. It was to be a lasting attitude. But other factors must have helped. There was, for example, simple geography; anywhere that mattered (culturally speaking) was a long way away. Then there was China's virtual economic and technological self-sufficiency. This was the result not only of rich natural resources, but of the fact that by Han times Chinese agriculture and technology had already provided the methods and devices needed to exploit the Chinese

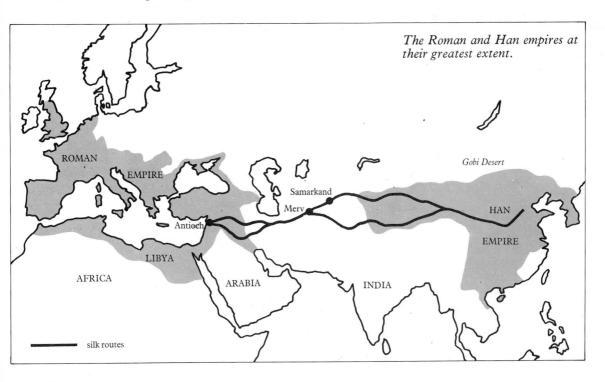

The Roman and Han empires at their greatest extent.

ROMAN
EMPIRE
Gobi Desert
Samarkand
Merv
HAN
Antioch
EMPIRE
LIBYA
AFRICA
ARABIA
INDIA

——— silk routes

environment successfully. Nothing obviously superior was available elsewhere. Rice, introduced in very early times from either southeast Asia or India, was the last really radical innovation in material life from outside before modern times.

Under the Han there were further refinements and inventions. Han scientists produced the first magnetic compass, with dial and pointer (though it was not used for navigation, but for laying out temples with the correct orientation) and the first system of cartography based on a grid system. They built machines to record earthquakes and provided their craftsmen with callipers with decimal graduation. In retrospect, though, of all the innovations of the period, the most striking is the discovery of how to make paper (announced in AD 105 from the imperial workshops). This was to be of enormous importance to the human race; it was cheaper and easier to make than papyrus or parchment (though it also deteriorated more rapidly than the latter). Knowledge of paper-making was not to reach the west for several centuries.

Transport and communications also benefited during Han times. The rudder attached to the stern of a ship – as opposed to a big paddle, hung over one side – appeared in the first century BC; it was not used on European ships for about twelve hundred years after this. It was also under the early Han that a breast-strap harness was developed for horses; far heavier loads than before could be drawn with it. A little after the end of the dynasty, the Chinese were to introduce the stirrup – an invention of enormous importance in warfare because of the greater security and control it gave to the rider.

Such innovations bear witness to the richness of Han civilization, and in many ways it was only the opening of a glorious period;

Left : a bronze horse cast during the later Han dynasty.

Right : this fragment is probably the oldest piece of Chinese silk in existence. It was made in about the fifth century BC, and is thought to have been taken to Altai (now well inside the Soviet Union) by a Chinese princess at the time of her marriage. It was preserved in deep-freeze – in the ice of a frozen tomb.

Chinese science and mathematics in the next thousand years were to throw up more new ideas by far than European. For the rulers and the rich, Han China at its peak must have been a splendid society. Some of its loveliest physical creations have perished; they were made in silk, wood and paint, and when palaces began to be burnt in the troubled last decades of the dynasty, priceless collections were destroyed. Still, many beautiful things survive because of the Han practice of burying the rich and noble with many of their possessions, or with models of them. One particularly notable recent discovery has been the jade suits in which a former Han prince and princess were buried. Under the later Han, bronze objects, especially models of horses, show a new development of one of the oldest Chinese arts, bronze-casting, while new coloured glazes were invented by the potters.

In much of Han art Chinese civilization

already seems deliberately to be looking backwards rather than to the future. This was true of the life of the mind too. Under the Han the scholarly writing of dynastic histories began, and the greatest of Chinese historians, Ssu-ma Ch'ien, wrote his *Historical Records*, highly esteemed by specialists in these matters. But the most important cultural development was the establishment of Confucianism as the official ideology of the state. This was in part because scholars naturally wished to restore the ravages caused to Chinese learning and libraries by an attempt of the Ch'in to destroy all books except those with a practical use or praise for the doings of the Ch'in. As the scholars worked, they rediscovered Confucian texts. It was in part also the result of deliberate policy. The Han emperors established professorships of Confucian studies, ordered regular sacrifices to Confucius in all government schools and began the practice of admitting recruits to the civil service on the basis of examination in the Confucian classics.

This was to be of enormous importance for the future of China; competitive examination was to give it an amazingly able though conservative bureaucracy right down to the twentieth century. But it was not enough to ensure the survival of the Han dynasty when faced by severe internal and external challenges. The most serious were more and more frequent peasant rebellions. Because of the growth of population, many peasants were landless and unable to find money for taxes and food. At the same time, there were renewed barbarian attacks from the outside. Warlords who controlled the professional soldiers on which the dynasty relied tended to seize power at home; barbarians, brought within the frontier in the hope of converting them to Chinese ways, turned on those who had brought them in. It was to the son of the greatest of the warlords that the last Han emperor resigned his throne in AD 221. When he did so, China fell apart again.

India

All that is left of the first account of a visit to India by someone from the West are some fragments quoted by later writers, but they are the first direct reporting about that country which exists. Alexander the Great had never got farther than the Punjab, and from the Greek accounts of his campaigns all that emerges is a muddled picture of little north-western kingdoms. We know that there was then a more important state called Magadha, in some sense dominating the lower Ganges Valley, but what it was like is very hard to say. So even scraps of what was said by a Greek ambassador sent to India in about 300 BC by the Seleucid king are of great importance. Megasthenes (that was the ambassador's name) travelled as far as Bengal and Orissa and tells us something about almost the whole of northern India.

Once we have set aside tall stories about people who lived on smells instead of food, and others with feet so large they could use them to keep the sun off, a picture emerges of an India ruled by a great emperor, Chandragupta, founder of a dynasty called the Maurya. His realms included not only the two great river-valleys but also much of Afghanistan (taken from the Seleucids) and Baluchistan. From his capital at Patna he ruled peoples divided, broadly speaking, into two religious traditions – one the old Brahmanical religion which was the root of Hinduism, and the other, apparently, Buddhist.

Chandragupta's son and successor began to extend the Maurya empire farther south. But it was the third Mauyra emperor, Asoka, who completed the process and finished by ruling over a larger area of India than was ever to be under one government again until the height of British power in the nineteenth century. Under his reign we at last begin to have fairly full documentation and can follow the story of Indian history in some detail. He left many in-

One of the pillars erected by Asoka, on which he set out texts. Asoka inscribed pillars not only because they could be seen from some distance, but because they reached to the sky and symbolically united heaven and earth. This one is in Delhi.

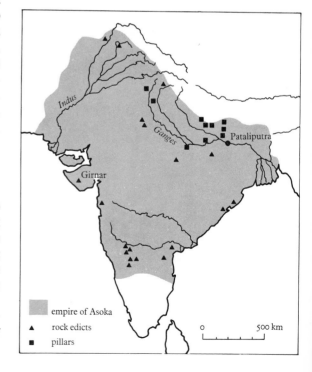

empire of Asoka
▲ rock edicts
■ pillars

0   500 km

scriptions, recordings, decrees and messages to his subjects, and these suggest Persian and Hellenistic influences; India was more closely in touch with the outside world than China. At Kandahar (one of the many cities named after Alexander the Great) Asoka left inscriptions in both Greek and Aramaic.

By Asoka's day India was firmly organized on caste lines. Over it ruled Asoka's bureaucracy, helped out, it seems, by a large secret police or internal intelligence service. Besides the duties we might expect it to carry out – gathering taxes, keeping public order, supervising irrigation, for example – this government machine had the task of promoting a set of beliefs, an ideology, we might say. Asoka himself was a Buddhist (he is said to have been converted after witnessing and being horrified by an especially bloody battle), but the message proclaimed on many of the inscribed pillars he left behind is not merely Buddhist. The ideas on them are summed up in the word *Dhamma*, a derivation from a Sanskrit word meaning 'Universal Law'. They recommended religious toleration, non-violence and respect for the dignity of all men. This is a very surprising set of ideas for an ancient empire. Probably these precepts – they were not set out as laws or decrees to be obeyed and enforced – were in part an attempt to make it easier to govern such a huge, ramshackle collection of many peoples, creeds and languages. 'All men', says one of Asoka's inscriptions, 'are my children'. It would certainly have made government much easier if everybody could have been brought to agree.

Asoka seems to have tried to put these principles into practice in public works likely to benefit all his subjects. Reservoirs were built, wells were dug, rest-houses put up at regular intervals along the roads of the empire and banyan trees were planted to give shade to travellers. But this does not seem to have overcome India's divisions.

Instead some of her most important religious distinctions seem to have deepened and hardened during Mauryan times. This can be seen at several levels. Religious ideas and literature, for example, took a step towards the crystallization of Hinduism, because this was when two great Indian epic poems, the *Mahabharata* and *Ramayana*, tales of gods, demons and historical derring-do, began to take their final form. To the first was now added a very important extension, the *Song of the Lord* (*Bhagavad Gita*). This was to become the central document of Hinduism, as important to them as the New Testament is to Christians. But more popular and superstitious cults also flourished in Mauryan times, and one of them was connected with the *Bhagavad Gita* very closely, for it was the cult of the most popular of all the Indian gods, Krishna, who is also the subject of the poem.

Buddhism prospered too under Asoka, though perhaps in the main because the emperor supported it. He even sent missionaries abroad. Those in Egypt and Macedonia did not do so well as others in Burma and Ceylon; in that island Buddhism was to remain the dominant religion from this time.

Many of these developments outlasted the Mauryan empire, which began to break up soon after Asoka's death. Why this happened is not clear, but perhaps the simplest explanation is that it outgrew its resources. In any case Indian society was in large measure independent of political regimes. Because it was organized on lines of family and caste, what happened above their level did not much concern the average Indian. Like the Chinese, Indian empires could not fall back on much loyalty if they ceased to deliver the goods in terms of order and well-being.

Caste, family and religion provide the long continuities in Indian history. And the economy did not alter much either. In many ways the life of the Indian peasant can have changed very little between Mauryan times and the arrival of Europeans in the sixteenth century

AD. Perhaps this was inevitable given the climate and the routines it imposed. Yet there were some important developments in Indian society about whose origins we do not know much, but which must lie at least as far back as Mauryan times. There is, for example, the growth of trade. This mattered to government because of the revenue brought in by tolls – hence, perhaps, the attention to road-building. A growth of commercial and industrial guilds accompanied this and went so far that some guilds were regarded as threats to the authority of the king. Foreign trade too, with both Africa and the Roman empire, was growing all the time.

The last Mauryan emperor was assassinated (in about 184 BC) and after that Indian history dissolves into a very confused story for about five hundred years. One or two things stand out in the muddle. First in importance is a series of invasions from the north-west. The Bactrians, descendants of the Greeks left behind by Alexander the Great on the upper Oxus, were the earliest intruders, pushing into the Indus Valley in the first century BC. They were followed by other peoples who at different times set themselves up in the Punjab. One group, very interesting but mysterious, were the Kushanas. They had migrated all the way from the borders of China and always seem to have had their main interest focused on Central Asia, but they ruled an empire which at

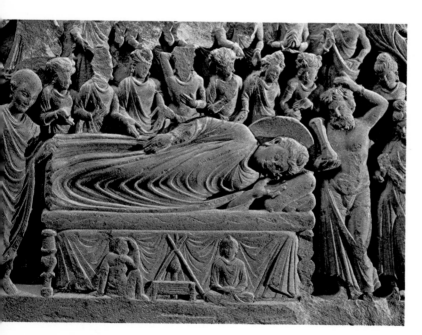

A stone relief shows Buddha during the fourth great event of his life, nirvana. He is not dead, nor has he reached eternal life; he is lying in a state of un-utterable bliss.

Right: Shiva was the Destroyer in the trinity of Hindu gods. He is sometimes portrayed with several heads to show the different aspects of his nature.

one time stretched from the steppes to Benares on the Ganges.

The Kushanas were keen Buddhists. It was in their time that sculptured images began to be made of the Buddha (often in a style which shows Greek influence). This was one illustration of the way in which Buddhism was coming down to earth, to be a religion like other religions. But many changes were taking place at the same time, and all the Indian religions and sects show interplay with one another.

The Kushanas went under in due course, and India again dissolved into a jumble of kingdoms. Political unity did not reappear until a new empire, the Gupta, was founded in AD 320; that story can wait to be told elsewhere.

What can be distinguished in Indian history above the confusion of the centuries during which the Han ruled China and the Roman empire was at its height is the continuing importance of invaders from the north-west. They brought new influences yet never overcame the continuing and growing power of Indian traditions and ways to absorb them. The newcomers always tended to be Indianized after a time. Nor did they ever really penetrate the south. After Mauryan times, indeed, that area was not to be united again to the north in a political whole until the British Raj. It was to remain the region where Hinduism was most strongly entrenched and conservative.

Above: a sacred stupa (gravemound) in Ceylon. The stupas were erected in memory of the Buddha and his saints, and the whole structure of the building had significance. The stupa was enclosed by a stone fence with four gates; the base of the building represented the earth, while the domed roof was the sky.

Right: the eastern gateway to the great stupa at Sanchi in central India.

The Roman empire

Imperator (which we usually translate as 'emperor') was a title borne by Augustus and his successors. It first meant simply someone commanding an army. Then it began to be applied to successful generals as an honour – a reward for winning victories. The Caesars then began to use it as an honorific title whether they had won battles or not. Only at the end of all this did it come to mean what we think of as 'emperor': the man at the top of the empire. Much of the history of the empire was like this; as had happened under the Republic, institutions and ideas changed gradually and in almost unnoticed ways in the short term.

In the century after Augustus' death there were twelve emperors, of whom the first four were related to him or his family. The last, Nero, died in AD 68. At once the Empire dissolved in civil war; four emperors were proclaimed in a year. What this showed was that, when an emperor was not able to assure his chosen successor a peaceful takeover, real power lay with the army. In fact this had already been so under the Julio-Claudian family; now it became obvious because of the upheavals of the 'Year of the Four Emperors'. There might even be more than one army to take into account, when provincial garrisons supported different candidates, and sometimes the Praetorian Guard at Rome itself might have the last word, because it was on the spot. The Senate still appointed the first magistrate of 'the Republic', but could only manoeuvre and intrigue if conditions were favourable; it could not defeat the soldiers in the last resort. As for the emperors themselves, provided they kept the soldiers with them, their personal characters and abilities would decide what sort of impact they produced.

A good emperor emerged in the end from the Year of the Four Emperors. Vespasian's worst fault seems to have been stinginess. He was far from being a Roman aristocrat (his grandfather had been a centurion turned tax-collector) but he was a distinguished soldier. The old Roman families had now clearly lost their grip on power, but Vespasian's own family – the Flavians – were not able to keep the hereditary succession going for long and the second-century emperors went back to Augustus' solution of adopting heirs. Four of these, the 'Antonine emperors', gave the empire almost a century of good and quiet government, looked back on later as a golden age. Three of them were Spaniards, one was a Greek. So the empire now did not belong to the Italians either.

Cosmopolitan at the top – as the diverse origins of the emperors showed – the empire was also breaking down barriers between peoples at the bottom. The Romanization of leading families in the provinces went ahead steadily. Young Gauls, Syrians, Africans and Illyrians all learnt Latin and Greek, wore clothes like those of the Romans and learnt to think of *Romanitas* – the Roman heritage – as something to be proud of. Meanwhile the civil servants and army held the structure together, respecting local feeling so long as the taxes came in regularly. When a decree gave the rights of citizenship to all free subjects of the empire in AD 212, this was the logical outcome of a long process of assimilation. By then even senators were sometimes non-Italian by birth. To be 'Roman' was by then not to have been born in a particular place, but to belong to a particular civilization.

The prestige of the emperors' office grew. Less and less did they resemble the 'chief magistrate', and more and more did they look like oriental kings, different in kind from their subjects. This was helped by the custom of regarding the emperor as a god. Julius Caesar and Augustus had both been deified after death; with Vespasian's son, Domitian, emperors began to be made gods while they were still alive. Particularly in the East, altars on which sacrifices had been made to the Republic or Senate were now reattributed to the emperor.

Those who regretted such changes could hardly deny that the empire was an astonishing achievement and one in which Romans could take pride. To provide regular, lawful government over a wider area than ever before, to black, white, brown 'Romans' equally, and thus to provide the empire's subjects also with the blessings of peace and the prosperity it brought – all this was without precedent and remains the best ground for saying that the Romans did great things.

And, of course, it was not all they did. At lowlier, more material levels, they left great monuments behind. The most obvious is still their building and engineering. Centuries later, men explained Roman ruins as the work of long-departed giants and magicians, so amazing did they find them. This was as mistaken as the English seventeenth-century antiquarian who said that Stonehenge was a Roman temple; it *must* have been, he thought, because only the Romans could possibly have done anything so grand. Yet these mistakes are understandable. What the Romans left behind in brick, stone and concrete was of enormous impressiveness and long unrivalled in the West.

Most of it had very practical aims. No legion was supposed to camp even for a night without digging itself into a properly planned and defensible camp with ramparts, so that the army

The extensive ruins of Colonia Marciana Thamugadi (modern Timgad in Algeria) give a clear picture of the layout of a Roman town. Many temples, basilicas, theatres and streets have been excavated from the sand.

The castle of St Angelo, Rome, Hadrian's tomb.

A Roman theatre at Merida in Spain, typical of the fine buildings erected in all the provinces of the empire.

got plenty of practice in surveying, engineering and building. Most Roman building, though, was in towns. All over the empire public buildings and monuments showed what the Romans thought appropriate to civilized living. To service the towns, the Romans built the roads which linked them and provided the arenas, baths, drains and fresh-water supplies to make them comfortable. They liked magnificence and produced some vulgar things, but they were practical; they did not build anything so useless as the pyramids. Some of their tombs were very grand, though; that of the Emperor Hadrian became the castle of St Angelo in Rome.

The Romans did all this with a very efficient but not very novel technology. They had better tackle than the Egyptians, as well as windlasses, cranes and iron tools which the builders of the pyramids had never had, but not much that was not already known to the Greeks. They used a wide range of materials, but most were already available. The exception was concrete, which they invented. It made possible the building of quite new shapes. The Romans were the first architects to get away from the need to hold up broad spans of roof with lines of pillars: they invented the dome supported on vaults.

The spectacular aqueduct of the Pont du Gard, built 63–13 BC to bring water to Nîmes.

Right: El Djem Colosseum in Tunisia, modelled on Vespasian's famous Colosseum in Rome. The amphitheatres were built with underground passages through which animals were driven onto the floor of the arena out of the openings which can be seen on the left.

Part of the heating system of the hot room of the baths at Bath, with a fragment of mosaic pavement. The floor was supported on columns or piles, and heat from a furnace below ground level passed between the piers supporting the floor, and thus warmed the room.

Lavatories were provided in rooms at the public baths. These examples are from Sabratha in Libya.

Some of the most visible Roman remains now left to us are roads. Occasionally their surfaces are still good enough to carry traffic, and even where they have disappeared, the routes they followed are often still followed by modern roads. A special corps of surveyors kept up the skills which made possible the astonishing accuracy with which Roman roads went straight across hill and vale, but the donkey work of building them was usually done by the legions. They gave the empire the swift communications which made possible the government of so wide an area. Between the age of the Caesars and that of the railway train there was no improvement in the speed with which messages and goods could be sent overland – and in some places communication got much worse in the next thousand years when Roman roads were not kept up.

Roman ruins provided huge quantities of ready-cut stone for later builders all over Europe. The damage done makes it difficult now to imagine just how splendid much of the empire must have looked. Some great single monuments remain – the Pont du Gard in the south of France; the arena at Nîmes, not far away; the Black Gate at Trier; the aqueduct still bringing water to Segovia, in Spain; or the complex of baths at Bath, in England. In many more places all over Europe, the Near East and North Africa there are fragments. At Pompeii there is a whole town to see. Above all, there survives the astonishing wreckage of imperial Rome itself.

The Romans prided themselves on being tough and hardy, but they also liked comfort. Sometimes they overdid the business of self-indulgence (as the lists of what was served at the great feasts of the rich when big parties were fashionable show). Their enjoyment of bathing and central heating is more easily excused. They used wisely their great skill in all matters of plumbing and sanitation. Elaborate aqueducts (the one at Segovia is still in use) brought drinking-water to the cities with-

in which public baths and lavatories looked after the cleanliness of the outer and inner man. In private houses, steam-rooms and living-rooms were centrally heated from under the floor. Not until the twentieth century did the inhabitants of Britannia again get used to the idea of properly heated houses.

Away from engineering and hydraulics, Roman innovations were fewer. There was little Roman contribution to pure science. In agriculture, watermills were just beginning to be introduced towards the end of imperial times; windmills had not made an appearance. Muscles, animal and human, remained the main source of energy.

Some people have suggested that it was because large numbers of slaves were available that the Romans did not need to invent labour-saving machines. There may be something in this, but other explanations are possible. There was the enduring problem of turning an idea into a practical invention, given the state of technology. Increasingly, too, the empire's history forced rural estates to try to be self-sufficient; they got by on what they could do for themselves, and did not try experiments. Finally, there was no stimulus from outside; China's treasury of technical skill was too far away, and Rome's immediate neighbours had nothing very impressive to offer her.

A detail from a family monument in the first century BC *shows one of the technological appliances in use at the time: some slaves are working a treadmill to hoist a sepulchral column by crane. Such cranes were in use well into medieval times.*

Right: some technology has changed very little over the centuries. This plumbline and set square were in use in ancient Rome.

Pompeii

In AD 79 Pompeii was a town which would nowadays be thought small (it covered about eighty hectares) but which was in the eyes of its citizens and of other Romans a place of some importance. Its history went back to Etruscan times and its inhabitants – there were about 20,000 of them – were descended both from pre-Roman stocks and from Roman colonists who had settled there when Rome's power was extended over the rich and fertile Campania. It stood on a river, the Sarnus, which is now of no importance, but which then allowed Pompeii to serve as a port for trading vessels which picked up agricultural produce and goods made in the town. Pompeii was one of the centres through whose markets and wharfs the Campania was in touch with the outside world, and so it was a thriving and important place.

Towering over the surrounding countryside – it rises about 1200 metres above sea-level – was Vesuvius, the last volcano still to be found active on the mainland of Europe. The little city lay about nine kilometres from the summit and about six from another city, Herculaneum, on the coast due west of the volcano. Vesuvius is a survivor of several ancient volcanoes in the region; a few others on near-by islands (like Etna in Sicily) have also remained active. Vesuvius last erupted in 1944 and, given the historical record and the frequency it shows, there seems to be a good chance that it will break out again before very long. But the most disastrous and famous of all its eruptions took place on 24 August 79.

The details are remarkably well known because we have an eye-witness account from the younger Pliny. For some days there had been earthquake tremors in the area. Springs had dried up – signs of increasing pressure within the mountain. Then, probably a little before mid-day on 24 August, there was a great explosion. A new crater opened in the mountain and a blast of hot gas hurled thousands of tonnes of rubble, much of it red-hot, thousands of metres high. This went on for some time. An umbrella-like cloud (which must have looked somewhat like that caused by a nuclear

A street in Pompeii with Vesuvius in the distance.

explosion) blotted out the sun. Then the debris began to rain down on the surrounding countryside.

By mid-afternoon Pompeii was buried under five to six metres of pumice stone and ash. Herculaneum escaped this, but was instead engulfed by scalding mud which buried it fifteen metres deep and eventually set as hard as rock. This happened slowly enough for people to escape: only twenty or thirty skeletons have been found there. In Pompeii the story was different: about 2000 died in the city, some struck down by stones but more, probably, gassed or suffocated as the ash piled up around them. Many other towns and villages near by were obliterated too. In an hour or two a whole society was wiped out. Pompeii was to remain virtually undisturbed, an entombed city, until in 1763 its site was at last identified after fifteen years of excavations.

The plaster cast of a watchdog which had been chained up and died of suffocation when buried by ash and cinders, which then hardened around the corpse. Once the corpse had disintegrated, a hollow mould was left, from which the cast could be made.

Right: this wall painting found at Pompeii shows an official seeking popularity by making a free distribution of loaves.

The peristyle (colonnaded court) of a villa in Pompeii, the House of the Vettii. Many of these houses were richly decorated with mosaics and wall paintings.

Some of the larger, less formal gardens had their own vineyard, and some houses even had their own fuller's workshop. This wine-press was found in a house in Pompeii.

A carving of a chariot race. Along with gladiatorial games, chariot races became more and more popular under the empire. The emperors and other rich men arranged increasingly lavish spectacles to gain popularity.

There were several different types of gladiatorial contest. This bronze statuette is of a gladiator who fought in traditional Samnite armour. The Samnites had once been Rome's toughest enemies in central Italy, and it had taken many years to defeat them.

Below: not all prisoners who came face to face with a fierce animal in the arena were free to tackle it or even to defend themselves. On the left a Libyan prisoner is tied to a stake in the chariot from which he attacked the Romans, and a panther is springing at him.

This carving from a grave in northern Gaul shows peasants paying taxes. They are wearing the local dress of the neighbourhood in which the tomb was found.

As for more abstract arts, certainly Rome did not produce philosophers such as those of classical Greece, but neither did anybody else, the Chinese and Indians included. The Hellenistic philosophers were not such original thinkers as their predecessors. As it was, the Romans produced some good expounders of Stoic philosophy, historians of note, and a galaxy of writers of Latin prose and verse, among whom Virgil, the epic poet, is unquestionably a giant figure even in world literature. The intellectual activity the Romans seem most to have admired after literature is, characteristically, a practical one – the law, and the oratory that went with it.

It is easy to run down the Roman intellectual achievement by comparison with that of Greece. But it should be remembered that to have produced for centuries such a succession of conspicuously able all-rounders suggests that the reliance of Roman culture on conservative ideas and the Greek tradition had much to be said for it. Roman politicians who reached the top were for a long time likely to have to act for long periods as administrators, generals, supervisors of building and engineering works, advocates and judges. Their culture produced men in abundance who could do all this. And the kind of empire they ran was a tolerant, cosmopolitan one, in which even so revolutionary a creed as Christianity, with all its implications for future upheaval, could take root and flourish. That was an intellectual achievement too: it was a Christian empire that went back to trying people for blasphemy.

The inscription on the forum at Wroxeter, England, dedicating it to the emperor Hadrian from the people of the area. This inscription is in what is known as monumental writing, which was a type of lettering easily chiselled evenly into stone. The Romans would use one of two other forms of writing when using a pen or stylus. Of course very few examples of these remain, as they were written on more perishable materials.

Christianity and the empire

The Christian Churches which soon emerged all over the Roman world were independent of one another. Everyone recognized that the Christians at Jerusalem, where the first generation of the Church's leaders had actually known and heard Christ, deserved special respect. But the only links between all Christians were the rite of baptism (which was the sign of acceptance into the new faith), their belief in the risen Christ, and the ritual of the 'eucharist' – the special service which re-enacted and commemorated Christ's last meal with his disciples on the eve of his arrest, trial and crucifixion.

Most Christians also long believed that the end of the world was not far off. They thought that Jesus would soon return to gather up those faithful to him and assure them salvation at the Last Judgement. If you believed this, then clearly there was not much to do here and now except watch and pray. Running the Churches was not therefore a very complicated business. Still, as they grew in numbers and wealth, there were administrative decisions to be taken, and so there appeared officers called bishops and deacons. They were to continue, but took a much more sacerdotal role as time went on, concerning themselves more with the conduct of worship and questions of theology.

Another important change was that Christianity soon broke almost completely with Jewry. It never shed its essential inheritance from Jewish culture – its monotheism, the Old Testament books of the Bible, and its view of human destiny as an extension of the special pilgrimage of a chosen people through history – and the Christian culture remains soaked in ideas and images drawn from the Jewish past. Nonetheless it broke with Jewish society and the Jewish nation. The Romans long thought of Christians as just another Jewish sect, but the building up of gentile Churches made them distinctive. Jewish Christians failed to convert their people to their view that the long-awaited Messiah of his people had come in Jesus. They could hardly go on attending the synagogue when it was known that they associated at common meals with gentiles who ate pork, were uncircumcised and did not observe other features of the Jewish law.

Another turning point was reached when a great Jewish rising against the Romans in Palestine broke out in AD 66, when the future emperor Vespasian was the local commander there. This was the worst Jewish rebellion the Romans ever had to master. After seven years' fighting, the reduction of Jerusalem by starvation to the point at which its inhabitants had turned to cannibalism to survive, and the destruction of the Temple (rebuilt after the return from the Exile and so known as the second Temple), the last Jewish forces committed mass suicide rather than surrender their stronghold at Masada in AD 73.

The Christians had not joined in the revolt, and this may have made the Roman authorities less suspicious of them. But neither had other Jews outside Palestine. Therefore, though Jerusalem was taken from the Jews after the revolt (Hadrian made it an Italian colony in 135 and excluded all Jews from Judaea), elsewhere they were still treated differently from other subjects of the empire, and were left much to themselves under the government of their own religious authorities. Still, the revolt and its aftermath made the Jewish people even more self-conscious and reliant upon the observations of the strict Law, since the Temple was again no more. This made the Jewish Christians' position still more awkward.

It was only somewhat later than this that the Romans persecuted Christians seriously. To

Left: the Romans saw their defeat of the Jewish rebellion of AD 66 as a great triumph and commemorated it in reliefs on the Arch of Titus in Rome. Here the Menora (seven-armed candelabra) from the sacked Temple is being brought in procession to Rome.

Below: the Jewish stronghold at Masada had been built by Herod the Great about a century before the tragic end of the Jewish rebellion. It is now a shrine.

begin with, it was the Jews who did so; they had demanded the crucifixion of Christ, had killed the first Christian martyr (St Stephen) and had given St Paul his roughest moments. Some scholars have even blamed Jews at Rome for bringing down on the Christians the first Roman (and local) persecution, by pointing them out as scapegoats for a great fire at Rome in AD 64. Many Christians in the capital perished horribly in the arena or were burned alive, and legend says that both St Peter and St Paul died in this persecution.

Terrible as this was, it was unusual; Christians seem usually to have enjoyed official toleration until well into the second century AD. Tales were told about them by the suspicious – they were said to practise black magic, cannibalism and incest, and some Romans disliked the way that their religion encouraged Jack (or Joanna) to think himself as good as his (or her) master in the eye of God and therefore to resist the traditional authority of husbands, parents and slave-owners. It was easy for the superstitious to think that the Christians were the reason for natural disasters – the old gods were angry that Christians were tolerated and so sent famines, floods, plagues, it was argued. But this did not much affect officials or the law.

The empire only came officially into conflict with Christianity in the second century, when it was discovered that Christians would refuse to sacrifice to the emperor and the Roman deities. The Romans could accept a similar refusal from the Jews as a distinct people with customs to be respected. But the Christians were not in the same position: why should they not carry out these acts of formal respect like other people? Condemnations followed for those who refused – not for being Christian, but for refusing to do something the law commanded. This no doubt also encouraged unofficial persecution; in the second century there were bad pogroms or popular

Even before Christianity broke away from Jewry there were sects with unorthodox beliefs among the Jews. At least one sect expected the imminent arrival of a liberating Messiah and in recent years evidence about it has come to light in the 'Dead Sea Scrolls'. Some of these scrolls, not found until 1947, seem likely to have been written by contemporaries of Jesus.

harryings of Christians in many parts of the empire, notably in Gaul.

Yet this century was also one of advance for the Church. The first of the great figures called the 'Fathers' – theologians and administrators who laid down the main lines of Christian doctrine so as to distinguish it more and more sharply from other creeds and to make more precise the duties and obligations of Christians – belong to this age. Among them are usually numbered two who were particularly important for the way in which they tried to connect Christian and Greek ideas (and therefore to help separate Christianity even more clearly from a mass of other oriental cults), St Clement of Alexandria and his pupil, Origen.

Great as were their intellectual and moral achievements, some features of the age favoured the Fathers. For one thing, whatever hostility was shown to them, Christians lived in a religious culture; a great search for new ways in religion was going on all over the Roman world in the second century, and Christianity profited from it. Moreover any new idea could spread quickly in a world held together by Roman law and order, where people could travel freely and everywhere find others speaking Greek, the common language of educated men. By the end of the third century about a tenth of the population of the empire may already have been Christian, one emperor had been (at least nominally), and another seems to have included Jesus Christ among the gods honoured privately in his household. In many places the local authorities by then expected to deal officially with the local Christian leaders, who were often prominent in their communities and, as bishops, played a large part in their affairs and represented them.

Underground burial grounds, called catacombs, were used as a refuge by Christians in times of persecution and later became places of pilgrimage. Those shown here – in Rome – are the most extensive surviving.

Parthians and Persians

In 92 BC a Roman army reached the Euphrates. For the first time the Republic was in direct contact with the Parthians, a people who were to play an important part in their affairs for the next three centuries. Nearly forty years later this became only too obvious when a Roman army invaded Mesopotamia and was within a few weeks wiped out in one of the worst military disasters of Roman history. Evidently the Parthians were not to be lightly interfered with. Who were they?

In origin they were another of those nomadic Indo-European peoples who had come down from Central Asia into the highlands of Iran somewhere about 1000 BC. They were famous for their way of fighting on horseback, appearing to flee but then turning in the saddle to shoot arrows as they galloped off – hence the term 'Parthian shot'. But this was not all that marked them out. They had also chosen to settle just south-east of the Caspian, in an area later crossed by a major caravan route from Asia to the Levant – the Silk Road from China. In due course this would bring important revenues to the Parthian kings. There they lived, first under Persian rule, then under the Seleucids until in the middle of the third century BC the local Parthian governor had enough of Seleucid rule and decided to strike out on his own. This was the beginning of the independent Parthian kingdom which was to last for nearly five hundred years.

It was broadened in the next century under two great brothers, both called Mithradates. They acquired a Parthian empire which at its greatest stretched from Bactria in the east to Babylonia and the Euphrates frontier with Syria (all that was left by this time of the Seleucid kingdom) in the west. Even Chinese emperors thought it worthwhile to open up diplomatic relations with Parthia (possibly, among other things, because of the fame of the splendid Parthian horses, much prized in China).

The two Mithradates called themselves on their coins 'Great King' and 'King of Kings'; these were the traditional titles of the rulers of Persia. In using them, they were claiming that they inherited the authority of the great Achaemenid rulers whose empire was destroyed by Alexander. Yet early Parthia was probably very loosely organized. It may have

A Parthian archer on horseback.

Imposing ruins of what was once the capital of the Parthians, Ctesiphon.

been more like a coalition of great noblemen bringing their contingents to the army of their overlord than a centralized and well-organized state. Still, by the time the Romans met it, the Parthian army was a formidable machine. Besides its traditional mounted archers, it had an arm the Romans lacked, the heavy armoured horsemen called 'cataphracts', whose mounts, like them, were clad in chain-mail.

Rome and Parthia tended to quarrel over Armenia, a frontier kingdom east of Anatolia which both thought of as falling into their sphere. There was a series of ding-dong struggles, with each side sometimes victorious, and at one time a Roman army actually occupied the Parthian capital at Ctesiphon, but the frontier did not change much. The disputed area was too far away for Rome to be able to hold conquests there without great effort and expense, and the problems of the Parthian kings at home were too distracting for them to think of expelling the Roman threat from Asia altogether.

True, we do not know very much about the internal affairs of Parthia, but that is partly because the records are poor – perhaps a sign that things were not going well inside the monarchy. Nor do we know dates very exactly, though we know that in about AD 225 the last Parthian king was killed by one of his vassals who was ruler of Fars, or 'Persia'. The man who overthrew him founded a new empire, ruled from Ctesiphon. His name was Ardashir (Greek-speakers called him Artaxerxes). The Sassanid empire (it was named after one of his ancestors, Sasan) which he launched was to be Rome's greatest antagonist. His descendants would make the splendour and grandeur of the Achaemenids live again and were to restore Persian supremacy in much of the Near East.

Ardashir and the other Sassanids strove to emphasize their continuity with the Persian past. Their empire was officially Zoroastrian in religion, as the Parthian and Achaemenid

Sassanid kings – like Assyrian and Persian kings before them – were often depicted as hunters to illustrate their boldness. This alabaster relief of a king hunting lions dates from the end of the fourth century AD.

A portrait of Ardashir on a gold coin.

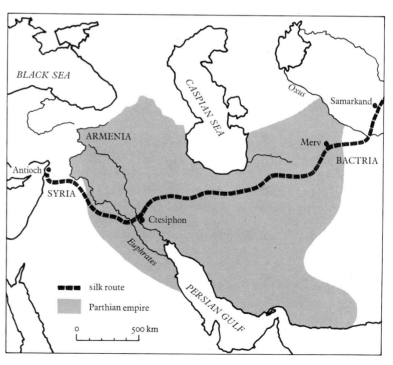

silk route

Parthian empire

0   500 km

regimes had been, but somewhat more uncompromisingly so. Ardashir claimed too all the lands ruled by Darius, the greatest Achaemenid, and used the old Persian kingly titles. The traditions of Sassanid bureaucracy went back even farther, to Assyria and Babylonia, and so did the royal claim to a divine authority. Not that this went uncontested. In so far as the Sassanid empire had any internal politics they were about struggles between the monarchy and the great noble families who claimed descent from old Parthian chiefs. These wanted to keep power in their own hands and sometimes even to interfere with the succession to the throne. But, though sometimes successful, they had to face a king with the powerful supports of a professional army paid for by taxation and the Zoroastrian priesthood.

Under the Sassanids a united Persian empire was to outlive its old rival, the Roman, after centuries of conflict. But they were also centuries of exchange, when Persia passed to

Persian rulers after the Achaemenids

330 BC Alexander overthrows last Achaemenid emperor and rules Persia until his death in 323.

305 BC Seleucid rule begins in Persia. The Seleucid emperors retain control until a Parthian emperor, Mithradates I (171–38), ejects them.

171 BC Mithradates I comes to the throne and begins the rule of the Arsacid dynasty over Persia. They retain power until AD 225.

AD 225 Ardashir I opens the rule of the Sassanid dynasty, which retains the throne until the last of the line is killed after Arab invasions in AD 651. Persia then passes to Moslem rulers.

the West important contributions of its own to be taken into Rome's cosmopolitan civilization. For a long time, though, this was less obvious than the threat presented by Persia. This threat was all the more dangerous because it first appeared at a moment when Rome was handicapped by threats elsewhere and by confusion in her own internal affairs. Between AD 226 and 379, for instance, while only nine Sassanid kings ruled in Persia and the empire therefore had the advantages of long reigns and the stability that went with them, there were thirty-five Roman emperors.

Shapur I (241–72) was perhaps the most outstanding of the Sassanids, at least until almost the end of his line. He once took captive a Roman emperor (Valerian, poor man, who was said to have been skinned alive and stuffed by the Persians, though this may not be true), conquered Armenia and invaded the Roman provinces of Syria and Cappodocia several times. After Shapur's reign there were longer periods of peace between Rome and Persia, but the two great powers never settled down to live easily together. In the end there came to be further divisions between them than existed at the start, because the Roman empire became officially Christian and that meant that the struggles of the two empires had an ideological side too.

A tomb at Naqsh-i Rustam is decorated with the scene of the emperors Philip and Valerian submitting to Shapur I.

The imperial frontiers

The Roman empire was at its greatest extent when the emperor Trajan died, in AD 117. It then covered an area about half that of the modern United States. It would have been an uncomfortable trip for some of the way, but a man could have walked from north-west Spain to the Persian Gulf without leaving Roman territory except for a brief sea-crossing from Thrace to Asia Minor. Armenia had been annexed in AD 114, and this took Rome's frontier to the Caspian in the north-east. The big province of Dacia, north of the Danube, had been conquered a few years earlier.

Some of these lands (notably those across the Euphrates) were almost at once to be given up by Hadrian; still, even without them, this was a huge area. Clearly it posed big security problems, though, once the Punic wars were over, only in the East was Rome threatened by a great power – a state like Rome itself, capable of putting big armies into the field and carrying out long-term diplomatic and strategic plans. There, Parthia and Sassanid Persia were successive challengers, but they had no equivalents anywhere else. On the other hand, problems of a different kind always faced the Romans elsewhere, and these grew harder to deal with as time passed. Africa was almost the only place where affairs stayed reasonably quiet after the acquisition of Mauretania in AD 42. This was in large measure because Rome had no African neighbours who much mattered; no large native populations lay just beyond the limits of Roman rule – there was only desert. In Europe things were very different.

An example of the awe-inspiring Roman road system. This road connects Antioch and Aleppo, and was built during the reign of Trajan.

All along the frontier from the Black Sea to the mouths of the Rhine were peoples belonging to stocks we call 'Germanic', with whom the Romans were often at war. Some of them had been thrown out of their original homelands by the Romans. They could be formidable opponents. Augustus had hoped to extend the limits of the empire to the Elbe, but it had become clear that this would not be possible – not least because of a great disaster in AD 9 when three legions were entirely wiped out (this defeat affected Roman morale so badly that the numbers of the destroyed legions were never allowed to reappear in the army list). Because of the problem presented by these peoples, an elaborate frontier – or, as the Romans called it, *limes* – had been created.

The *limes* was not just meant to show where one government's responsibilities ended and another began, as do boundaries between most states today, but to protect what lay behind it and to separate it from something else. If there is a modern parallel, it was rather like the modern frontier between East and West Germany. The Roman *limes* separated two different states of culture. On one side of it were Roman order, law, prosperous markets, fine towns – civilization, in short. On the other were tribal society, technical backwardness, illiteracy, barbarism. Of course, complete insulation was impossible and there was always a certain coming and going. Still, the Romans saw the frontier as something they looked out from warily, not as a stage on a journey leading somewhere else.

Where possible, it was based on natural obstacles. In continental Europe, for example, it followed the lines of the Rhine and Danube. Along them were dotted permanent legionary camps and these were linked by signal towers and smaller strongpoints. Roads ran along the frontier so that troops could be marched quickly from point to point. In gaps between natural obstacles fortifications were built of

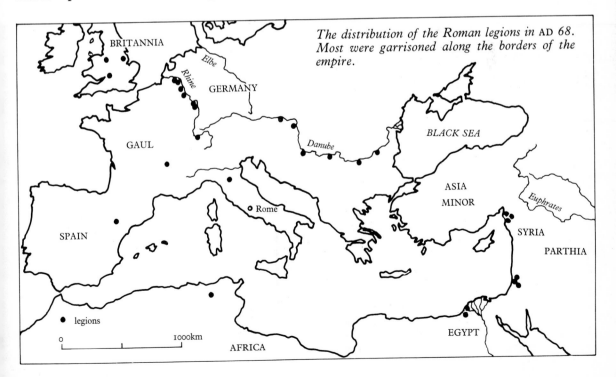

The distribution of the Roman legions in AD 68. *Most were garrisoned along the borders of the empire.*

turf, timber or sometimes masonry. One long stretch of works of this sort ran between the upper Rhine and Danube, and another in the Dobrudja ran down to the sea. The most remarkable of all these artificial frontiers was begun in about AD 122 in northern Britannia, between the Tyne and Solway Firth. This was the work known as Hadrian's Wall, after the emperor who built it. It was eighty Roman miles long (about 120 km) and was in its final form a masonry wall, protected on both sides by ditches some ten metres wide and three deep. Sixteen forts were distributed along it and smaller strongpoints were placed at intervals of a mile, with two turrets between each strongpoint. This was the most elaborate of all the Roman frontiers and the most developed form of the *limes*. It well illustrates the purpose described by Hadrian's biographer – 'to separate the Romans from the barbarians'.

Even such defences as these, though, were not effective unless well manned. The danger from the barbarian Scots and Picts was shown by what happened when the Romans dropped their guard. Twice, once at the end of the second century and once during the fourth, a temporary weakening of the garrison led to the Wall being overrun, and when this happened

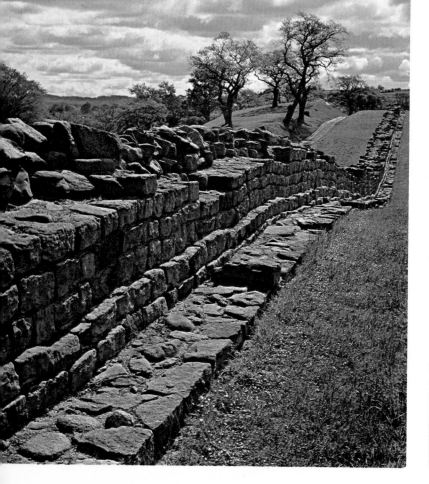

Left : part of Hadrian's Wall in Cumbria. On the south side of the wall there was usually also a vallum or rampart of earth flanked by ditches.

Below : in the first century AD the Romans built two lighthouses at Dover, only one of which now remains. These lighthouses were used as watchtowers as well as guides for ships.

the invaders swept far into the south, pillaging and destroying. There was, however, one difference from the frontiers in continental Europe, in that these people do not seem to have sought to settle in Roman territory.

For a long time, the Rhine frontier was thought to present the greatest threat. Eight legions were kept there on a comparatively short stretch of the frontier. By Augustus' day the army was a long-service force, based on volunteer recruits, more and more of whom were drawn from the provinces. They were often barbarians, but they served not only in specialist units with a local background – like the slingers of the Balearic isles, for example, who were especially skilled with their weapons, or the heavy cavalry of the Danube provinces – but also in the legions of infantry which were the core of Rome's military power. Usually there were twenty-eight legions – about 160,000 men in all – and they all served along the frontiers or in distant provinces like Spain and Egypt. (There were about as many troops again in auxiliary and specialist arms like the cavalry.) Long duty in the same areas tended to make the legions less mobile as the years went by; the garrison towns contained large populations of dependents and families who could not easily move (some became the sites of cities still flourishing today). But the great internal network of roads still gave the empire's commanders great advantages in moving their forces swiftly from one place to another. Gradually the balance of the army's dispositions was changed; by the early third century half the Rhine legions had been removed, while the army on the Danube had been doubled in size.

This all added up to a pretty formidable division of cultures in Europe, and it affected future history. For one thing, it did much to shape the way in which Christianity came to pagan Europe. It also defined a 'Latin' Europe, cutting it off from the northern and trans-Danubian Germanic societies (the Slav peoples had not yet come on the scene). Even the shape of future European nations was to owe much to the divisions Rome imposed within the Germanic world by drawing frontiers as and where she did.

The Vandals were a Germanic tribe, originally from the southern shores of the Baltic, who by the fifth century AD had overrun north-west Africa. This mosaic, from their African capital of Carthage, shows a Vandal leaving his villa. Many of the German barbarians soon took up Roman ways.

Diocletian and Constantine

Soon after AD 200 the Germanic peoples were pressing harder and harder on the frontier, demanding to cross and settle within it. Some of this was attraction by civilization and wealth. But there were also more fundamental forces at work. Probably they were under pressure from other peoples to the east, who in turn were propelled westwards by changes in Central Asia, whether natural (such as climate) or political (such as the disturbance of the Hsing-Nu, or Huns, by the Han emperors). A sort of shunting was going on, and at the end of the line the Germanic tribes were bumping into the Roman frontier.

Given strains and diversions elsewhere, it was impossible to hold them off for ever. The barbarians may never have attacked in large force at any one place or time – they seem to have been able to put a maximum of twenty or thirty thousand men into the field at once – but they were too strong for the third-century empire. First some of the Rhenish tribes were allowed to settle in Roman territory (where they were then recruited to help defend the frontier against further arrivals). In the east the Goths crossed the Danube in 251 (and killed an emperor in battle); five years later the Frankish peoples crossed the Rhine. Another group, the Alamanni, were soon raiding as far south as Milan. Meanwhile the Goths went on to Greece and then began to harry Italy and Asia Minor from the sea.

This was a terrible time, made all the worse because the barbarian onslaughts were going on while within the empire a new period of civil war and disputed successions had begun. When the last Antonine was murdered, there was another four-sided struggle for the throne. Many third-century emperors were killed by their own troops; one fell in battle to his own commander-in-chief, who was then slain by

the Gauls after being betrayed to them by one of his own officers. Crushing taxation, economic recession and soaring inflation meanwhile struck at people far removed from such exalted circles as these; local bigwigs began to be unwilling to serve as town-councillors and officials when such posts meant only that they would have to incur unpopularity by collecting heavier taxes – often in kind, as the monetary crisis grew worse. One sure sign of trouble was the rebuilding of many cities' defensive walls in the second half of the century. They had not been needed under the Antonines, but now even those of Rome were put in order and towns which had never been fortified were given defences.

At the end of the century luck changed, in that once again a succession of able emperors came to the top. They were of Illyrian stock, and the first to turn the tide was Aurelian, 'Restorer of the Roman Empire' as the Senate appropriately called him. He was murdered as he was about to invade Persia, but his successors were good soldiers too. Nearly ten years after his death another Illyrian came to the throne who was not only to re-create (at least in appearance) the old power and glory of the empire, but was actually to bring about a revolution in the way it operated.

Diocletian came of humble origins. He was very traditionally-minded and had a very exalted view of his role. He took the name 'Jovius', for example – Jove or Jupiter, the Roman name for the king of the gods, the old Greek Zeus – and seems to have seen himself as a god-like figure, supporting single-handed the civilized world. This no doubt has something to do with his decision to persecute Christianity, the creed whose adherents refused to sacrifice to the gods and emperors. Respect for these gods had carried Roman arms to success in the past; why, then should not the Christians comply? This was not a new question.

By the time he began to deal with it, Diocletian had provided what might seem to a modern observer (though not necessarily to a Roman) many more practical remedies for the empire's troubles. One – an attempt to peg prices and wages and so halt inflation – was a disaster. Probably the most important step he took was one whose full implications he may not have seen: more than any other single man, Diocletian opened the way to a division of the empire into two separate entities, East and West, which would go separate ways. Whether this outcome, or something like it, was bound to occur has been much debated. Alexander's empire (or much of it) in the Hellenized East and the western Greek world the great conqueror had never visited had been welded together by Rome, although there were always differences between them. But it was only in the difficult third century that it began to seem impossible to deal with the problems of the West when the resources of the richer East were needed against the barbarians and Persians.

Diocletian's reform was an attempt to deal with the danger of civil strife and over-extension. In AD 285 he divided the empire along a line from the Danube to Dalmatia and appointed a co-emperor to the western half. The co-emperor, like himself, had the title Augustus; each of them also had an assistant, nominated his successor, called a Caesar. Other changes followed. The Senate's small remaining powers disappeared; to be a senator was now only an honour. The old provinces were divided into smaller units called 'dioceses', which were governed by imperial nominees (the governors of the provinces had been appointed by the Senate from its own members). The army was regrouped. It was much enlarged too; conscription was brought back, and soon there were about a half million men under arms.

This by no means solved all problems, though it undoubtedly helped to pull things together. The machinery for assuring a quiet succession of Augusti only worked once, when Diocletian and his colleague abdicated in AD 305. (Diocletian retired to his enormous palace at Split, on the Yugoslav coast, whose ruins enclose much of the modern town there.) A bigger army meant more taxation, to be paid for out of a smaller population.

Yet the long-term results were very important. The division of the empire on Diocletian's plan was not stuck to by his successors, and there were again to be single-handed

A Roman gold medallion showing the emperor Diocletian. Right: Diocletian's palace at Split.

This head of Constantine was originally part of an enormous seated statue of the emperor more than ten metres high. The size of the statue hints at the later Byzantine trend towards emperor-worship.

attempts to rule it as a whole. Nonetheless, there had been an important practical division in administration, and every future emperor had to accept a large measure of subdivision in practice.

A part of the effort to pull the empire together – and it must show that people were no longer taking it for granted or feeling loyalty to it in quite the same way – was an even greater emphasis on the unique, almost divine authority of the emperor himself, its oriental side in fact. This was to be very important for the future of Christianity, for in the first place it boded ill for the old Graeco-Roman tradition of religious toleration. It was in 303 that Diocletian launched the last general persecution of Christianity. It did not long outlast his abdication two years later, though kept up a few years longer in Egypt and Asia than in the West. Paradoxically this was just on the eve of the first great worldly triumph of the Church, its acceptance as the official religion of the empire.

This was the work of the emperor Constantine. He had first been hailed as emperor by the army at York in 306 and reunited the empire in 324 after two decades of civil war. He had soon decided to see if the Christian's god would help him. There is no reason to doubt his religious sincerity – he seems always to have hankered after a monotheistic creed and for a long time worshipped the sun-god whose cult was associated with that of the emperor. In 312, on the eve of an important battle and as a result of what he believed to be a vision, he ordered his soldiers to put on their shield a Christian monogram by way of showing respect for the Christians' god. He won the battle. Soon afterwards toleration and imperial favour were given to Christianity. Constantine went on to make gifts to churches – though his coins still for many years bore the symbol of the sun – and took part in the internal affairs of the Church by giving judgement at the request of the parties in an important dispute over its affairs in North Africa.

One can sense from his acts that Constantine moved only gradually towards personal conversion. From 320 the sun no longer appeared on his coins and his soldiers had to go to church parades. In 321 he made Sunday a public holiday (though he said this was out of respect for the sun-god). He built churches and encouraged converts by giving them rewards and jobs. Though he never formally disavowed the old religions and cults, he finally declared himself a Christian. Like many other early Christians he was not baptized until he was on his deathbed, but he presided in 325 over the first ecumenical council of the Church – one attended by bishops from the whole Christian world – at Nicaea. This founded a tradition that the emperors had a special responsibility as rulers who united religious and lay authority; it was to last right through the European Middle Ages.

Constantine made one other contribution to the future when he decided to settle his capital at Byzantium, an old Greek colony at the entrance to the Black Sea, to be known as Constantinople. He wished to build there a city to rival Rome itself, but one unsullied by pagan religion and it was to remain an imperial capital for a thousand years. But it was in making the empire Christian that he shaped the future most deeply. He did not know it, but he was founding Christian Europe. He deserves his title – Constantine 'the Great' – though, as has often been said, because of what he did rather than why he did it, or what he was.

The Chrismon, an early symbol (seen here in the first two lines of text) used by Christians, is made up of the Greek initial letters of the word Christ.

Right: following the Council of Nicaea, another Council was held at Constantinople in 381. An important statement of faith to be repeated by believers was approved there and is still in use. This ninth-century painting shows the Council at work.

Decline in the West

The eastern empire continued to grow away from the western, and the effect in the West was profound. The East was more populous, could feed itself and could raise more taxes and recruits; the West grew poorer, its towns slipping into decline, and depended on importing corn from Africa and the Mediterranean islands and, in the end, on barbarian recruits for defence.

Gradually the imperial capital in the East came to rival Rome and even outshone it. Christianity too emphasized the separation of two zones: the Latin-speaking West had two great Christian communities within it, the Roman (presided over by their bishop, the pope of Rome) and the African. They were increasingly different from the Greek-speaking Churches of Asia Minor, Syria and Egypt, all of which were more receptive to oriental influences and more influenced by Hellenistic tradition.

Constantine's sons ruled the empire until 361. Soon after, it was divided again between co-emperors and only once more, under Theodosius, were East and West ruled by one man. Symbolically, he was the emperor who finally forbade the worship of the old pagan gods, thus putting the empire's force behind Christianity and in effect breaking with the old Roman past. But by his day things were already going downhill still faster in the West, and by 500 the western empire had vanished.

It may be best here simply to emphasize at the outset *what* happened, rather than why. The whole of society was not suddenly engulfed as if by an earthquake. The main thing that disappeared was a machine, the Roman state – or, rather, what remained of it.

In the fourth century the western empire's administration had been seizing up as more demands were made on its dwindling resources. No conquests could be made to help pay for defence. As taxes went up, so more people left the towns and sought to live self-sufficiently in the country to avoid them. Less money meant a poorer army, and that meant more reliance on barbarian mercenaries – which cost still more money. Concessions to them had to be made just as pressure was building up from a new wave of migrations.

In the last quarter of the fourth century a particularly nasty nomadic people from Asia, the Huns, fell on the Gothic peoples who lived on the Black Sea coast and the lower Danube, beyond the Roman frontier. The eastern empire bungled the peaceful settlement of refugees within the frontier and the Visigoths turned on the Romans. In 378 they killed an emperor at the battle of Adrianople and soon cut off Constantinople by land from the West as more and more of them flooded into imperial territory.

A few years later and the Visigoths were on the move again, but towards Italy. Another barbarian general, a Vandal who had been taken into the imperial service, stopped them. From 406 the empire was employing barbarian tribes as 'confederates' (*foederati*) a word which meant barbarians who could not be resisted but who could be persuaded to help. This was the best the West could now do for its defence, and it was not enough.

Soon the barbarian peoples were wandering the length and breadth of the old West. In 410 came the sack of Rome by the Goths, an event so appalling that it led St Augustine, an African bishop who was the greatest of the Fathers of the Church, to write a book which was to become one of the masterpieces of Christian literature, *The City of God*, in order to explain how God could allow such a thing to happen. The Visigoths eventually got as far as Aquitaine in south-west France before coming to terms with the emperor, who persuaded them to help deal with the Vandals, who had by then overrun Spain. Under Visigothic pressure, the Vandals in the end crossed the Straits of Gibraltar and settled in North Africa, making their capital at Carthage. There they remained, dropping across the Mediterranean in 455 to sack Rome a second time.

Terrible as this was, the loss of Africa was worse for the western empire, whose economic base was now narrowed to little more than part of Italy. It was hard to say exactly when the empire ceased to be there. The names and symbols – like the Cheshire cat's smile – were the last things to go. When the Huns were finally turned back from the West at a great battle near Troyes in 451, the 'Roman' army was made up of Visigoths, Franks, Celts and Burgundians – all of them barbarians – commanded by a Visigothic king. When, in 476, another barbarian king killed the last western emperor, he was recognized with the title 'patrician' by the eastern emperor.

For all the forms, though, the reality was that the western empire had by now been replaced by a number of Germanic kingdoms,

and 476 is usually reckoned as the date at which a line can be drawn under the story of the empire which began with Augustus. But there are no simple endings in history, and many of the barbarians (some by this time educated by the Romans) saw themselves as the new custodians of a Roman authority which went on. They looked to the emperor at Constantinople as their ultimate sovereign. By the end of the fifth century many of them had settled down beside the old provincial gentry of Gaul, Spain and Italy, adopting Roman ways; some of them were even Christian. Only in the British Isles did the barbarians almost completely obliterate the old Roman past. These are things to discuss elsewhere. Evidently, though, we are not at the end of the story of ancient civilization, whatever happened to the empire.

Centuries earlier a Roman poet had remarked of one of Rome's conquests that 'Captive Greece took her wild captor captive'. He meant that, though the Greek states had gone under, the triumphant Romans had been overcome by Greek civilization. Something a little like that happened in the West as the Roman empire came to an end.

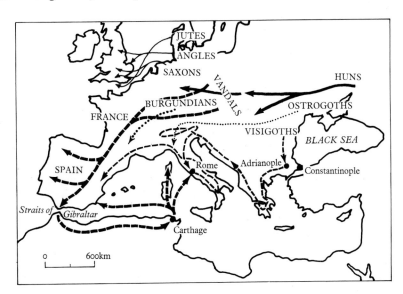

Some of the routes probably taken by the barbarian invaders during the fifth century AD. *By the end of the century the western empire had almost entirely fallen to the invaders – but the eastern empire was to survive for another 1000 years.*

Conclusion

As the behaviour of many barbarians suggests, Romans – and through them, Greeks and Jews – did not stop influencing history in 476, or at any other date. There was to be a 'Roman' empire based on Byzantium for almost a thousand years (its story is important too and must be told elsewhere), and even in 1800 there was still something called the 'Holy Roman Empire'. Christian clergymen were then still wearing a costume based on that of the Roman gentleman of the second century AD. Paris, London, Exeter, Cologne, Milan and scores of other towns and cities were all still important centres of population, just as they had been in Roman times, even if there had been centuries during which they had been much less prosperous than under the Antonines. Much of the map of Europe had still the shape the Romans had given it by their choice of garrison towns and communication centres, and often their settlements had reinforced the effect of natural divisions.

Even today the continuities are there, though perhaps the non-material ones are more obvious. First and foremost comes language: the European languages are packed with words from Greek and Latin, the tongues through which the Bible first came to Europe. Our ways of counting and dividing time too come from the Graeco-Roman world. It was Julius Caesar who took up the suggestion of an Alexandrian Greek that a year of 365 days, with an extra day every fourth year, would be better than the complex traditional Roman calendar, and it was under Constantine that the Jewish idea of a Sabbath day of rest once in seven became accepted. And, of course, it is to early Christianity that we owe the distinction of BC and AD on which the whole Christian and most of the non-Christian world still works today. (Soon after 500 a monk first calculated the date of Christ's birth; he was in error by a few years, but his decision has remained the basis of our calendar.)

Many more examples could be given – from Greek mathematics, Roman law, Christian theology, to take only a few – of ideas from antiquity with great historical influence before them. As people came to look back in later times, they were much struck by what they owed to the civilization which produced them. But they also took something else from that past. Most civilizations have classical ages from which they draw the standards by which to assess later achievements. This was perhaps the most important role for the future of the civilization whose story we have been following in this book. Later Europeans sometimes exaggerated what the Greeks and Romans had done, but they found in it both an inspiration and a test of their own performance. Classical antiquity became a myth of what civilization could and men ought to be. This is why in a very deep and important way, Greece, Rome and Judaism are still at the heart of many of the ideals and beliefs of later Europeans. It explains why, like medieval men, modern men too walk among the ruins of this great past and still find them amazing.

Time chart

BC

5000–2500 Neolithic peoples on Greek mainland (later called Pelasgoi)

c. **2500** Indo-European tribes invade Greece

c. **2400** Minoan civilization (to *c.* 1200)

c. **2000** China: Yu the legendary 'Great Engineer' founds Hsia Dynasty (to *c.* 1600). Early Greek-speaking tribes settle Greece

c. **1600** China: Shang Dynasty (to *c.* 1100). Hittites sack Babylon and flourish (to *c.* 1100)

c. **1250** The events remembered as Moses' leading of the Israelites from Egypt

1184 Trad. date, Fall of Troy (the seventh of nine cities of Troy)

1100–800 Dark Age of Greece. Dorians dominate Peloponnese, Melos and Crete, later settle Rhodes, Cos and Crete. Ionians settle S.W. coast Asia Minor

c. **1027** China: Chou Dynasty (to *c.* 256 BC)

1000–700 Greek-speaking Achaeans disperse around Aegean and settle self-governing communities. Geometric pottery

c. **920** Palestine a divided monarchy: Judah and Israel

c. **800** Carthage founded by Phoenicians. Homer: *Iliad* and *Odyssey*

776 Trad. date, first Olympic games

c. **750** Italy: Etruscan culture (Etruria); hut settlements on Tiber at crossing which is site of future Rome

c. **750** Greece united by common language based on Phoenician alphabet. Colonies set up: Marseilles (*c.* 600), Syracuse, Sicily (*c.* 728), Naucratis (*c.* 640), Cyrene (*c.* 630). Coins in use; warfare changed by hoplites; appearance of polis.

745–727 Assyria: Tiglath-Pileser III founds Neo-Assyrian Empire

c. **671** Assyrian conquest of Egypt (to *c.* 652)

c. **612** Assyrian Empire collapses; fall of Nineveh

c. **610** Lydian Empire in Asia Minor

600–500 Etruscans and Latins amalgamate to become first Romans. They trade with Celts

c. **594** Solon's code of law at Athens

586–538 Babylon: destruction of Jerusalem; the Hebrew Exile

539–331 Achaemenid Persia. Cyrus unites Medes and Persians, overthrows Babylonian Empire (*c.* 539), Median Empire (*c.* 549), Lydian Empire (*c.* 546), Zoroastrianism spreads throughout Middle East. Improved roads, decentralized government. Darius extends Persian Empire to India making the Indus valley a Persian satrapy. Xerxes I (485–464). Hellenization *c.* 332

516 Temple at Jerusalem rebuilt

c. **510** Last Etruscan king. Rome a republic

499–494 Ionian revolt

490–480 Persians attack Greeks (Marathon, Thermopylae, Attica, Athens, Salamis). Persians defeated as Plataea, Mycale (479)

481–221 China: Warring States period

480–380 Greece: golden age of philosophy, poetry, medicine, science, mathematics, literature, art, history, theatre, architecture, naval supremacy

478–404 Delian League and Athenian Empire

447–432 Construction of Parthenon at Athens

431–404 Peloponnesian War. Athens surrenders to Sparta

430–426 Plague at Athens

400–300 Greek states decline in power

399 Trial and death of Socrates

390 Rome sacked by Gauls

387 The 'King's Peace' on Persia's terms. Ionia abandoned to Persia

379–374 Renewed wars between Greek states. Thebes and Athens at war with Sparta. Athens makes peace with Sparta (374)

359 Macedonian Empire. Philip II gains control Greece (338). Alexander the Great, his campaigns against Persia (334–330) and N. India (329–326), siege warfare and phalanx, exploration, uniform coinage. With Alexander's death in 323, the Empire begins to disintegrate. It reforms into a group of big states with hereditary monarchies, the last of which rules Egypt (Ptolemies) until the death of Cleopatra, 30 BC

330 Persian Empire falls to Macedon

322 End of democracy at Athens

c. **320** India: Chandragupta Maurya. Caste system. Buddhism established, Graeco-Bactrian influence. Maurya Dynasty (to end of Asoka's reign, 232 BC)

c. **312** Seleucid Dynasty (to *c.* 65 BC). Palestine under Ptolemies

280–275 Pyrrhus, king of Epirus, N.W. Greece, in Italy

264–242 First Punic War against Carthage.

c. **250** Parthians and Bactrians gain independence of Macedonian Empire

221–207 China: Ch'in Dynasty

206 BC–AD **220** China: Han Dynasty. Empire extends to S. Manchuria, much of S.E. coast China and Annam

218–202 Second Punic War

c. **170** Parthian Empire. Mithridates I and II

168 Rebellion of Judas Maccabeus

149–146 Third Punic War. Carthage destroyed

c. **6** Birth of Jesus Christ

AD

c. **33** Jesus Christ crucified

40 Kushan Dynasty, north-west India. Emperor Claudius invades Britain

47–60 St Paul's missionary journeys

c. **117** Roman Empire reaches greatest extent

200–300 First era of Barbarian threats to Rome. Goths, Visigoths, Franks

221–589 China: Dark Ages. Three Kingdoms (AD 221–265); T'sin Dynasty (265–316); Northern and Southern dynasties (316–589)

225 Ardashir I (Artaxerxes) overthrows Parthians. Sassanid Empire (to 637)

285 Diocletian divides Roman Empire into East and West

300–400 Coptic Christians from Egypt convert Ethiopians

313 'Edict of Milan' gives Christians legal rights. Constantine converts to Christianity

316–490 Tartar invaders in China

c. **320** Under Constantine, Christianity becomes religion of the Roman Empire

320 India: Gupta Empire (to 480); decimal system invented. Classical Hinduism emerges. Buddhism spreads from Nepal to Tibet, China and Japan

324 Constantine reunites Roman Empire, moves his capital to Byzantium (Constantinople)

325 Council of Nicaea
350-476 The Empire in the West declines as barbarian
    pressure increases
363-77 Persian power revives under Shapur II
378 Theodosius forbids pagan cults
400-600 Huns invade India
406-9 Vandals, Alans, Suevi and Burgundians invade Gaul
410 Visigoths (Alaric) sack Rome. Roman soldiers leave
    Britain
415 Visigoths settle S. Gaul and Spain
432 St Patrick arrives in Ireland

439 Vandals take Carthage
450 Marcian, first emperor to be crowned by Church
451-2 Huns invade Gaul, Italy. Defeat of Attila near
    Troyes
455 Vandals sack Rome
476 Odoacer deposes the emperor at Rome and rules as
    representative of the emperor at Constantinople
481 Franks under Clovis complete conquest of Roman Gaul
488-93 Ostrogoths invade and occupy Italy
496 Clovis becomes Christian
c. **500** Angles, Saxons, Jutes settling in England

Acknowledgements

The author and publishers would like to thank the following for their kind permission to reproduce illustrative material:

American School of Classical Studies for p. 34 *above left*; Archivo Fotgraphico for p. 43; Bath City Council for p. 98 *above*; Bibliotheque Nationale for p. 63; Colin Bord for p. 114 *left*; the Trustees of the British Museum for pp. 3 *left*, 8 *left and right*, 19 *left and right*, 21 *left*, 36, 41 *below*, 44 *above*, 45 *below left*, 53 *left and above right*, 61 *right*, 64 *left and centre*, 102 *above left*, 110 *below*, 115, 117 *left*; Peter Clayton for pp. 67 *below left*, 74; Cleveland Museum of Art for p. 110 *above*; Ehem Stattliche Musseen, Berlin p. 46; Werner Forman Archive pp. 3 *right*, 7, 25 *above*, 101 *above right*; Susan Griggs (Jehanger Gazdar) for p. 27 *below*, (Adam Woolfitt) 73 *above*; Sonia Halliday for pp. 77 *centre*, (Jane Taylor) 105 *below*, (Prue Grice) 112, (Martine Klotz) 119 *right*; Robert Harding Associates for pp. 25 *below,* 31 *above and below*, 34 *left and above right*, 41 *above right*, 43 *right*; Claus Hausmann for p. 92 *left and right*; Hirmer Fotarchiv for pp. 18, 53 *below right*; Michael Holford for pp. 3 *left*, 15 *above and below*, 17 *below*, 21 *left and right*, 23 *right*, 29 *left*, 36, 41 *below*, 44, 45 *above and below right*, 53 *above right*, 57, 64 *left and centre*, 115; A. F. Kersting for pp. 37 *above*, 93 *right*, 97 *above*; William MacQuitty Collection for p. 88; Mansell Collection for pp. 13 *above and below*, 23 *left*, 30 *left* and *right*, 34 *right*, 42, 50 *left and right*, 51 *left and right*, 55, 58 *left*, 64 *right*, 67 *above*, 70 *above and below*, 71 *left and right*, 99 *above and below*, 103 *above*, 107, 118; Ministry of Public Building and Works for p. 103 *below*; National Museum of Athens for p. 34 *above right*; National Museum of Naples for p. 48; for p. 95 from *Nelson Atlas of the Classical World*; Photoresources (C. M. Dixon) for pp. 2 *left and right*, 14 *above and below*, 17 *above*, 20, 25 *above and below*, 27 *above*, 28 *right and left*, 33 *above*, 37 *below*, 41 *above left*, 48, 52 *above and below*, 53 *left*, 56 *above*, 61 *right*, 68, 72 *left*, 72/73 *centre*, 76 *right*, 77 *right*, 84, 85 *left above right and below right*, 89, 90, (C. M. Dixon) 93 *left*, 100, 101 *left and below right*, 105 *above*, 108, 114 *right*, 119 *left*; Rapho Agency (Chuzville) for p. 40; Ronald Sheridan for pp. 10, 33 *below left and below right*, 61 *left*, 65 *left and right*, 75, 76 *right*, 77 *left*, 82, 96 *above and below*, 97 *below*, 101 *above left*, 106 *below*, 111, 117 *right*; Scala for pp. 69, 81; the Trustees of the Wellcome Institute for p. 47; Roger Wood for pp. 60, 98 *below*, 102 *below*, 109.

The author and publishers would like to thank the following illustrators for the maps and diagrams: Kathleen King for pp. 6, 9, 22, 26, 29 *right*, 38, 54, 59, 67, 78 *top*, 80, 83, 87, 90 *below*, 110 *below right*, 113, 121; Connie and Ray Burrows for pp. 11, 39, 50 *below*, 52 *right*, 56 *below*, 60 *below*, 69 *below*, 78 *below*, 79 *below*; Edward Poulton for p. 35.

Index

r. = reigned
d. = died
fl. = flourished
c. = approximately

Achaeans, the, 10, 12, 16, 58
Achaemenids, 24, 26-7, 110
  end of the empire, 60, 108, 111
  Persian rulers, 111
Adrianople, battle of, 120
Aegean, the, 4, 8-11
  in Dark Ages, 12-13, 16
  Greek domination, 13, 22
  city-states, 58
Aeschylus (*c.* 525-456 BC), 51
Aesop (*c.* 620-560 BC), 42
Afghanistan, 60, 61, 62, 90
Africa, 86, 92
  and Rome, 75, 94, 112, 120, 121
agriculture, Greek, 8, 10, 40-42
  Roman, 65-6, 71, 99
Agrippa, emperor (*c.* 63-12 BC), 97
Alamanni, the, 116
Alexander the Great (356-23 BC),
    25, 108, 117
  his fame and reputation, 59, 61
  campaigns and empire, 59-62,
    (map), 59
  and Persia, 59-61, 111
  'Successor' states, 61-3
Alexandria, 58, 61-3
  Jews at centre, 81
Antioch, 62, 112
Aquitaine, 120-21
Arabia, 86
Archimedes (*c.* 287-12 BC), 63
architecture, link with sculpture, 51
  classical orders, 50, 69
architecture, Roman, 78, 79, 95-9
  roads, 98, 112, 113, 115
Ardashir (Artaxerxes), Sassanid
    emperor (r. 224-40), 110-11
Aristarchus of Samos, 63
Aristophanes (*c.* 450-388 BC), 51
Aristotle (384-23 BC), 49, 59
Armenia, 109, 111, 112
army, Chinese, 89
army, Greek, 'hoplites', 32, 33, 34,
    36, 56-7, 58
  Macedonian phalanx, 39, 58, 60

army, Parthian, 108, 109
army, Roman, 64-6
  the legions, 68, 71, 74, 78, 113,
    115
  conscription, 70, 117
  under the empire, 72-3, 94, 95,
    115
  and the Republic in decline, 73,
    75
  source of political power, 77, 94
  outposts, 113-15
  reforms of Diocletian, 117
art, Chinese (Han dynasty), 87, 88,
    89
art, Egyptian, 6, 43
art, Etruscan, 28, 29, 30, 31, 32
art, Greek, pottery, 13, 15, 21, 23,
    40, 41, 44; sculpture, 51, 63;
    Mycenaean palace, 11, 12, 16
Asclepios, 47
Asia Minor, 12, 16, 28, 49, 62, 120;
  Persian wars, 36, 59-60
  Roman frontier, 112
Asoka, Mauryan emperor (*c.* 269-
    32 BC), 90-91
Assyrians, 23, 24, 27, 111
Athens, 13, 14
  the Acropolis, 20, 33, 35, 48, 51,
    56
  population, 23, 42
  pottery specialists, 32
  citizenship, 33
  gods and goddesses, 35, 36
  and Sparta, 38
  democratic government, 39
  the Parthenon, 40
  commercial city, 42
  slave population, 42-3
  the Academy, 44
  cultural and political supremacy,
    46, 54
  the Erechtheum, 50
  drama festivals, 51
  and Peloponnesian war, 54, 56-7
Attica, 10, 12, 38
  silver mines, 42, 43
Augustus (Octavian), emperor
    (63 BC-AD 14), 76-7, 81, 113,
    115
Aurelian, emperor (212-75), 116

Babylon, 59, 60, 62, 80
  'Hanging Gardens', 24
Babylonia, 108, 111
Bactria, 62, 92, 108
Balearic isles, 'slingers', 115
Baluchistan, 90
barbarians, 16, 24, 113-16 *passim*,
    120, 121
  routes followed (map), 121
Bath, Roman baths, 98
Black Sea (the Euxine), 4, 6, 23,
    24, 120
Bombay, 27
Britannia (Britain), Roman
    invasions, 73, 74
  Hadrian's Wall, 114-15
Bronze Age, 9
Buddhism, the Buddha, 87, 90, 91,
    92, 93
Byzantium, 86, 118
  imperial capital, 119, 120, 122

Cadiz, 22
Caere, Etruscan city, 29
calendars, 14, 29, 122
Campania, 31, 100
Cape Sounion, Greek temple, 7
Carthage, 27, 36
  Punic wars, 66-8
  reconstruction, 69
  Vandal capital, 115, 121
Caspian Sea, 108, 112
Central Asia, 9, 86, 92, 108, 116
  trade routes, 87
Ceylon, 86
  Budhism, 93
Chalkis, 22
Chandragupta, Mauryan dynasty, 90
charioteers, 2, 5, 10, 14, 102
Ch'in, the, 86
  their attempt to destroy books, 89
China, 9, 86
  Han dynasties, 86-7, (map), 87,
    93, 116
  acriculture and technology,
    87-9
  Great Wall, 87, 88, 89
  Silk Road, 87, 108
  religion, 89
  and Parthia, 108

Christianity, 27, 86, 103, 115
  link with Judaism, 4, 83, 104
  beginnings, 82-4
  common beliefs, 104
  development of the Churches,
    104, 107
  becomes official religion of
    Roman empire, 118-19, 120
  Councils of Nicaea and
    Constantinople, 119
Christians, 79, 80
  persecutions, 104-7, 116-17, 118
  the catacombs, 107
  the Chrismon, 119
civil services, 62, 77, 89, 91
Cleopatra (69-31 BC), 62, 76
coinages, 19, 23, 32, 58, 67, 74, 77
Colonia Marciana Thamugadi,
  ruins, 95
Confucianism, 89
Constantine the Great, emperor
  (c. 280-337), 118-19, 122
Constantinople, 119, 121
Corcyra (Corfu), 54
Corinth, isthmus of, 10, 38, 54
Corsica, 66
Cos, 12, 47
Crete, 8, 10, 12, 58
Crotone, 47
Ctesiphon, capital of Parthia, 109, 110
Cumae, 29
Cyprus, 62, 73
  Mycenaean-style palaces, 10
Cyrus II, king of Persia (r. 559-
  30 BC), 24, 26

Dacia, 112
Dalmatia, 117
Danube, the, 4, 6, 112, 113, 115, 116
Dardanelles, 23, 36
Darius I, king of Persia (r. 522-
  486 BC), 24, 26
Darius III, king of Persia (r. 336-
  30 BC), 24, 26, 111
  death, 60
Delian League, 39, 66
Delphi, 14
  temple of Athena, 200
  oracle of Apollo, 20
Democritus, 'atomic' theory, 47
Diocletian, emperor, persecutes
  Christians (r. 284-305, d. c.
  313), 116-17
  reforms, 117

Dionysius, drama festivals, 50, 52
Domitian, emperor (r. 81-96), 95
Dorians, spread in the Aegean, 12,
  13, 22, 23
Dover, Roman lighthouse at, 114

education, of Greek boys, 44, 46, 47
  Socrates and, 48-9
  under Roman empire, 94
Egypt, 2, 5, 6, 9, 24, 46, 59, 75, 76,
  115, 118, 120
  Persian conquest, 24, 27
  New Kingdom, 27
  religion, 27
  position of women, 43
  cult of the pharaohs, 62
  astronomical papyrus, 63
  pyramids, 96
Elba, 29, 31
Eretria, 22
Etruria, 29
Etruscans, 28
  political organization, 29
  and Rome, 29-31, 64, 66
  and Greek settlements, 36
Euclid (fl. c. 300 BC), 63
Euphrates, the, 108, 112
Euripedes (c. 484-406 BC), 51
Europe, Roman rule, 73, 113, 115, 122

France, 23, 68, 73
  Roman aqueduct at at Nîmes,
    97, 98
Franks, 116, 121

Ganges, 90, 93
Gaul, Gauls, 73, 75, 95, 103
  sack of Rome, 66
Germanic peoples, 113, 115, 121
  Roman settlements, 116
Gobi Desert, 87
Goths, 116
  sack of Rome, 120
Greece, early invaders, 10, 12
  Dark Ages, 12
  self-governing cities, 12-13
  overseas settlements, 22, 32
  government by 'aristocrats', 32, 34
  government by 'oligarchy' and
    'democracy', 32, 34, 39, 57
  the polis, 34-5, 40, 49
  jury service, 34
  fear of Athens, 39
  patriarchal society, 44

Greece, (continued)
  fifth-century achievements, 46
  state of vassalage, 68
Greeks, 16
  achievements, 4, 46-50
  and agriculture, 8, 40, 41, 42
  religion, 20, 21, 35, 40, 84
  sea-travellers, 22
  'metics', 32, 42
  peasantry, 40, 42
  'thetes', 42
  and the family, 44
Gupta empire, 93

Hadrian, emperor (r. 117-38), 77,
  96, 112
  Wroxeter inscription, 103
  his Wall, 114
Hannibal (c. 247-182 BC), use of
  elephants, 67
Herculaneum, priests of Isis, 85
  Vesuvius, 100
Herod the Great (73-4 BC), 105
Herodutus (c. 485-25 BC),
  Researches, 49-50
Hinduism, 90, 91, 93
  Shiva, 92
  Krishna, 91
  Bhagavad Gita, 91
Hippocrates (c. 460-377 BC), 47
Hittites, 10
Holy Roman Empire, 122
Homer, 16-17, 21, 32
  importance to Greeks, 17, 44, 59
  learning by rote, 44, 46, 47
  recited by Socrates, 49
  Iliad, 16-17, 29
  Odyssey (quoted), 18, 19
Hsing-Nu (Huns), the, 87, 116, 120

Illyria, 94, 116
India, 9, 81, 86
  Parsees, 26-7
  invaded by Alexander the Great,
    60, 62, 90, 91, 92
  and Christianity, 86
  Mauryan dynasty, 90-2
  caste system, 91
  Dhamma principles, 91
  peasantry, 91
  invasions from north-west, 92-3
  see also Buddhism; Hinduism
Indo-Europeans, 10, 26, 108
  migrations, 24, 28
Indus, the, 60, 92

Ionia, 12, 13, 23, 36, 38
  and modern science, 47
Iran ('Aryran'), 24, 60, 108
Issus, battle of, 59
Italy, 31, 65, 66, 116
  Greek settlements in the south,
    22, 23, 27
  Etruscans, 28-30

Jaxartes, 60
Jerusalem, 83
  destruction of the Temple, 24,
    80, 104, 105
  rebellion of the Jews, 104, 105
Jesus (c. 6 BC-AD 30), birth, 80, 82, 122
  Last Supper, 81
  trial and crucifixion, 82, 84, 106
  belief in his resurrection, 82, 104
Jews, and Christianity, 4, 80, 104
  the Exile, 24, 80, 81, 104
  a chosen people, 81-9
  Roman rule, 81
  the Dispersion, 81, 82-3
  wait for a 'Messiah', 82, 104, 107
  death of Jesus, 84, 106
  rebellion against Romans, 104, 105
  persecution of Christians, 106
Judaea, 81, 82, 104
Judaism, 27, 81, 83, 87, 122
Julius Caesar (c. 100-44 BC), 122
  in Gaul, 73
  invasion of Britain, 73, 74
  character, 75
  murder, 76, 78

Kandahar, 91
Knossos, 16
Kushanas, 92-3

Laconia, 12
Leonidas the Spartan (r. c. 489 BC,
  d. 480 BC), at Thermopylae,
  36, 38
Leuctra, battle of, 57
Levant, 4, 13, 108
  trading ports, 9, 22
  Mycenaean period, 10
  Phoenician cities, 22
Libya, 6, 62, 73, 86
literature, memorized, 16
  importance of Homer, 16-17, 21
  Greek, 50-51, 52, 62
  Chinese, 89
  Indian, 91
  Roman, 103

Macedon, 10, 58, 60-61, 62-3
  the phalanx, 39, 58, 60
Mahabharata and *Ramayana*,
  (Hindu epic poems), 91
Manchuria, 86-7
Marathon, battle of, 36
Marcus Aurelius, emperor (r. 161-
  80), 77
Marius (c. 157-86 BC), 68
Masada, Jewish stronghold, 104,
  105
Mauretania, 112
Medes, 24
Mediterranean world, 4, 6, 8, 9,
  22, 23
  Persian domination, 24
  Roman rule, 64-5, 73
  Jewish 'Dispersion', 81
Megasthenes, travels in India, 90
Mekong Valley, Thai people, 87
Melos, island of, 63
Mesopotamia, 9, 46, 59, 62
  Roman invasion, 108
Minoan period, 9
Mithradates I (r. 171-38 BC), 108,
  111
Mithradates II (r. 124-87 BC), 108
Mongolians, 87
Mount Olympus, 21
Mycale, battle of, 38
Mycenaean civilization, 11, 12-13
  palace script, 16
  bronze dagger, 10

Naples, bay of, 22
Naqshi-i Rustam, tomb, 111
navy, Greek, 36, 38, 39, 56, 57
  Roman, 69, 74
Nazareth, 80
Near East, 9, 10, 62, 86
  Assyrian and Persian empires,
    24, 26-7
Nebuchadnezzar II, king (r. 605-
  562 BC), 24, 27
Neolithic people (Pelasgoi), 10
Nero, emperor (r. 54-68), 77
Nile, 6, 9
North Africa, 8, 22, 23
Nubian pharaohs, 27

Olympic Games, 14, 15
Origen (c. 185-254), 107
Orissa, 90
Oxus, 60, 92

Paestum, Doric temple, 50
Palestine, 24, 62, 104
  Seleucid rule, 80-81
  Jews, 80-84
Parthians, and Persia, 108, 110-11
  and Rome, 109, 111
  empire (map), 110
  Sassanids, 110-11
Patna, Mauryan capital, 90
Peloponnese, 10, 12
Peloponnesian League, 56
Peloponnesian war, recounted by
  Thucydides, 50, 54
  origins of conflict between
    Sparta and Athens, 54, 56
  Pericles' funeral oration, 55
  Persian involvement, 56-7
  results, 57
Pergamon, Turkey, 58, 62, 68
  Acropolis, theatre, 52
Pericles (c. 495-29 BC), 33, 46, 54
  funeral oration, 55
Persepolis, destruction, 25
  'Tripylon' staircase, 25
Persia, Persians, 23, 24, 26, 33, 58
  religion, 26-7
  war with Greece, 36-8, 56-7
  naval forces, 36, 38, 56
  battles (map), 38
  defeat by Alexander the Great,
    59-61
  Sassanid empire, 111, 112
  Arsacid dynasty, 111
  Arab invasion, 111
Persian Gulf, 60, 112
Philip II of Macedon (382-36 BC), 58
Phoenicia, 66
  alphabet, 16, 17
  sea-traders, 22
  cities, 27
Plataea, battle of, 38
Plato (c. 428-348 BC), 44, 48
  philosophy, 49
Pliny the younger (c. 61-113), 100
Po, river, 6, 29
Pompeii, 98
  bronze head, 3, 5
  Roman mosaic, 48
  household shrine, 84
  temple of Vespasian, 85
  destruction by Vesuvius, 100
  excavations, 101
Pontius Pilate (fl. 26-36), 82
Portugal, 73

Praxiteles (*fl. c.* 364 BC), 51
Priene, Turkey, Greek theatre, 52
Ptolemies, 62, 66, 76
Punjab, 90, 92
Punic wars, 66-8, 70-71, 112
Pyrrhus, king of Epirus (*c.* 318-
272 BC), his 'victory', 66
Pythagoras (*fl. c.* 532 BC), 47

Rhine, 4, 113, 114, 115, 116
Rhodes, Doric settlers, 12
Rhône, 6
Roman emperors, Julio-Claudian, 76
Flavian and Antonine, 76, 94,
116, 122
deification, 77, 95
deaths by violence, 77, 116
increased prestige, 94
Roman empire, 64-5, (maps), 78,
79, 87
political changes, 77
and Christianity, 84, 103, 104,
106, 107, 111, 118
mapped by Ptolemy, 86
civil war, 94, 118
citizenship, 94
achievements, 95-6, 98-9, 103
frontiers, 112, 116
distribution of legions (map), 113
the *limes*, 113, 114
division by Diocletian (East and
West), 117
union under Constantine, 118
decline in the West, 120-21
Roman Republic, 64-9, 94
Punic wars, 66-8, 70, 112
political decline, 71-3, 75
becomes an empire, 76
and Parthians, 108, 109, 112
Romans, 98, 103
and Green learning, 4, 68, 72, 73
compulsory mobilization, 30-31
government by 'patricians', 31, 65
religion, 36, 70, 79, 84
dress and occupations, 64, 65,
70, 71
citizenship, 65, 70-73, 95
peasantry, 65-6, 70
Rome, 27-31
myth of Aeneas, 29
Romulus and Remus, 30
first city-building, 30
Praetorian Guard, 77, 94
castles of St Angelo, 96

Rome, (*continued*)
arch of Titus, 105
great fire, 106
the catacombs, 107
sack of, 120, 121
Russia, 6

St Augustine, *City of God*, 120
St Clement of Alexandria, 107
St Paul (Saul) of Tarsus (d. AD 62),
83-4, 106
journeys (map), 83
St Peter, 83, 106
Salamis, naval battle, 38
Samarkand, 60
Sanchi, great stupa, 93
Sardinia, 66, 68
Saul *see* St Paul
science, 47-50, 63, 89
Scipio Africanus (237-183 BC),
67-8
Scythians, 24
Seleucids, 62, 68, 80-81, 90, 108, 111
Seven Wonders of the World, 24, 63
Shapur I, Sassanid ruler (241-72),
111
Sicily, 36, 62, 68
Greek settlements, 22, 23, 58, 66
Mt Etna, 100
slavery, 63
in Greece, 42-3, 44
in Roman era, 42, 64, 68, 70-71, 99
the 'pedagogue', 47
Socrates (*c.* 470-399 BC), 44, 48-9,
52
Sophocles (495-406 BC), 51
Spain, 6, 22, 67, 68, 73, 75, 112,
115, 121
Roman theatre, Merida, 96
aqueduct at Segovia, 98
Sparta, Spartans, 14, 23, 33, 39
at Thermopylae, 36, 38
'helotry', 39, 43
position of girls, 43
and Peloponnesian war, 54, 56-7
Split, Diocletian's palace, 117
Ssu-ma Ch'ien, *Historical Records*,
89
Stoicism, 63, 103
Sumer, 24, 40
Syracuse, 23, 56, 66, 68
Syria, Syrians, 9, 24, 59, 62, 82, 95,
108, 111, 120
stone head, 3, 5

Tarim Basin, 86
theatre, 50-53, 96
Thebes, 14, 58
destruction, 59
Theodosius, emperor (*c.* 346-95),
120
Thermopylae, battle of the pass,
36-8
Thessaly, 10
Thrace, 24, 36, 49, 112
Thucydides (b. *c.* 470 BC), 50, 56-7
Pericles' funeral oration, 55
Tiber, river, 28
Tiberius, emperor (r. 14-37), 76
death, 77
Trajan, emperor (53-117), 72-3,
77, 78, 112
Trier, Black Gate (Roman), 98
Troy (Ilium), Achaean siege, 16, 17
Troyes, battle of, 121
Tunis, 73
Phoenician tomb inscription, 17
Tyre and Sidon, 27

Valerian, emperor (r. 253-60), 111
Vandals, 115, 121
Vespasian, emperor (r. 69-79), 79,
94, 95, 97, 105
Vesuvius, destroys Pompeii, 100
Virgil (70-19 BC), 103
Visigoths, 120, 121

women, position in Greece, 43-5
the 'hetaira', 43
in Greek drama, 44, 51
Roman, 103
writing, disappearance of in Dark
Ages, 12
origin in scripts, 16
Phoenician alphabet, 16, 17
Greek, 29
Chinese script, 86
invention of paper, 88
Roman, 103
Wu Ti, 'Martial Emperor' (r. 140-
86 BC), 86-7

Zama, battle of, 68
Zoroaster, Zoroastrianism, 26-7,
110-11
Zend-Avesta sacred book, 26-7